Researching education policy:
Ethnographic experiences

the Tufnell Press,

London,
United Kingdom

www.tufnellpress.co.uk

email contact@tufnellpress.co.uk

British Library Cataloguing-in-Publication Data
A catalogue record for this book is
available from the British Library

ISBN 1872767 621
Copyright © 2006   Geoff Troman, Bob Jeffrey and Dennis Beach
The moral rights of the authors have been asserted.
Database right the Tufnell Press (maker).

First published 2006

Printed in England and USA by Lightning Source

Researching education policy: Ethnographic experiences

by
Geoff Troman
Bob Jeffrey
Dennis Beach

Acknowledgements

We thank those listed below for permission to reproduce the following copyright material:

Chapter (1) G. Troman (1996) 'No Entry Signs: educational change and some problems encountered in negotiating entry to educational settings', *British Educational Research Journal*, 22(2.): 71-88. Reprinted by permission of the author and publisher, Carfax Publishing Company, Abingdon.

Chapter (2) B. Jeffrey and G. Troman (2004) 'Time for Ethnography', *British Educational Research Journal*, 30(4): 535-548. Reprinted by permission of the authors and publisher, Carfax Publishing Company, Taylor and Francis Group.

Chapter (3) G. Troman (1999) Researching Primary Teachers' Work: examining theory, policy and practice through interactionist ethnography, in Hammersley, M. (ed) *Researching School Experience: Ethnographic Studies of Teaching and Learning*. Reprinted by permission of the author and publisher, Falmer Press.

Chapter (4) B. Jeffrey How to 'describe' ethnographic research sites, previously published as Come 'descrivere' i luoghi della ricerca etnografica, in Gobbo, F. (ed) *Etnografia, Dell'Educazione in Europa*. Reprinted by permission of the author and publisher, Edizioni Unicopoli.

Chapter (5) D. Beach (2002) The Deceptive Imagination and Ethnographic Writing, in Walford, G. (ed). *Debates and Developments in Ethnographic Methodology, Studies in Education Ethnography Volume 6*. Reprinted by permission of the author and publisher, Elsevier Ltd., Jai Books.

Chapter (6) D. Beach. (2001) 'Artistic Representation and Research Writing', *Reflective Practice*, 2(3): 313- 329. Reprinted by permission of the author and publisher, Routledge, Taylor and Francis Group.

Chapter (7) G. Troman. (2001) 'Tales from the Interface: disseminating ethnography for policy making', in Walford, G. (ed) *Ethnography and Education Policy, Studies in Education Ethnography Volume 4*. Reprinted by permission of the author and publisher, Elsevier Ltd., Jai Books.

Contents

Introduction

This co-authored book draws on the published work of three experienced ethnographers whose research projects have focused on the effects of education policy in the U.K. and Sweden. The book traces some of the factors and experiences involved in the process of the development of an ethnographic project focusing on policy developments—from planning, through analysis and writing, to outcomes in the form of methodological articles produced by the authors from their various researches. The book has an introduction and two sections.

We have utilised ethnographic methodology in our research focusing on teachers' work and how it is changing in response to economic, social and cultural pressures. We have chosen this mode of research, involving participant observation, interviewing and immersion in the field for extended periods of time, for sound reasons. What many of the empirical studies of teachers' responses show is that the effects of restructuring of schools and educational systems, and the responses of the teachers to the process are complex and contradictory. Teachers' reactions cannot simply be read off from official policy prescriptions. The pattern of actual restructuring awaits empirical developments. What is needed is detailed studies of what happens when policy reforms are introduced into individual institutions in order to discover 'what is going on'. Policy analysis reveals the nature of education policy at the macro (system/societal) level. However, we need to understand the implications the reforms have for teachers and how they are experienced at the meso (organisational) and micro (personal) levels. This will contribute to policy sociology and will add to our understanding of the processes and dynamics of social change.

Policy ethnography considers policy as a cyclical process and aims to provide an analysis of it in the various phases of the cycle. It offers too, a means of bridging the macro-micro gap since a study focused on the impact of a range of policies in the 'zone of implementation' will tend to expose the constraints and influences of wider societal factors on what teachers do. There is a need also to complement those theoretical studies which have sought to analyse official policy for restructuring teachers' work and its organisation with empirical work focused on how restructuring is being played out in practice. There is a crucial role here for an ethnographic case study approach. Generally, there has been a neglect of the experiences, perspectives and emotions of actors who are charged with the implementation of policy and the social, cultural, political, economic and emotional contexts in which it takes place. Ethnography is a prime means by which such factors can be understood.

Section i—Policy and the ethnographic process

Without gaining access to educational institutions ethnographic studies could not possibly proceed. In chapter one, therefore, we consider some of the issues which were encountered in gaining access to schools in order to carry out ethnographic work on policy implementation. In chapter two the focus is on the difficult dilemmas of how much time to spend in the field in order to gain immersion thus increasing the validity of the ethnographic account produced in the study. Ironically, ethnographic research on policy is constrained, in terms of time spent in the field, by the policies of research sponsors who often favour short-low-cost research. In chapter three it is noted that it is sometimes argued that ethnography in being focused on the local and particular might be macro-blind and unable, therefore, to contribute to the development of theory. We argue here, that interactionist ethnographic research on education can contribute to our understanding of theory, policy and practice.

Section ii—Policy, representation and dissemination

In this section we argue the strengths of the ethnographic approach in researching education policy, look at the ethnographic policy research process, and explore some of the issues it raises in terms of interpreting and communicating findings of enquiries. In chapter four the inter-related and complex issues of entry, access and interests are reflected upon and explored in the context of a U.K. National inspection. Once having obtained access the search for oppositional incidents, differing reactions and behaviours as well as contradictory data can ensure that the ethnography represents the lived complex reality and can also illustrate the existence of contradictory policy that confounds those at the sharp end. Chapters five and six deal with representations in ethnography. In chapter five a post-modern, post-structural perspective is used to deconstruct representational power and the politics of conviction in literary texts of the ethnographic kind and in chapter six the question of political and ideological articulation in relation to ethnographic writing style is examined. Finally, chapter seven renders the current official emphasis on producing research findings problematic, not solely to contribute to academic knowledge but to be of use to 'users'. Using the example from our research on stress in teaching we show how problematic is the shift towards more direct collaboration with users, and the highly contested nature of the relationship between ethnographic research, policy and practice.

Section I—Policy and the ethnographic process

Chapter 1

No entry signs: educational change and some problems encountered in negotiating entry to educational settings.

Geoff Troman

Introduction

For those embarking on ethnographic fieldwork a necessary first stage involves gaining entry to the setting which has been chosen for study. This vital phase of the research is encountered by novitiate and experienced researchers alike. Whether the focus of study is to be a formal organisational culture, like a school, or an informal culture such as a deviant group of adolescents, the researcher, in order to gain access to participants, develop field relations, collect and analyse data, must first successfully negotiate entry to the culture. This process typically involves the fieldworker negotiating with a participant who has authority in the setting, who is a prominent reality definer in the group, and who, acting as 'gatekeeper', has the power to grant or deny entry to the researcher. This power differential is, then, not to the advantage of the researcher, in this or any other stage of ethnographic fieldwork (Hammersley, 1996).

Gaining entry, however, is a stage in research which is not without its difficulties. Stephen Ball (1990a) reminds ethnographers that the art of gathering soft data is no soft option. This is so because in ethnographic fieldwork the researcher is the prime research instrument. Researchers in this tradition:

> ... stand alone with their individual selves. They themselves are the primary research tool with which they must find, identify, and collect the data. They must charm the respondents into cooperation. They must learn to blend or pass in the research setting, put up with the boredom and horrors of the empty notebook, cringe in the face of *faux pas* made in front of those whose cooperation they need, and engage in the small deceptions and solve the various ethical dilemmas which crop up in most ethnographies. (Ball, 1990a, p. 157)

Since in ethnographic studies the researcher is the 'primary research tool', entering the culture which is to be the focus of study is for the ethnographer high in 'risk, uncertainty and discomfort' (Ball, 1990a, p. 157). All of these threats are particularly heightened during the negotiation of entry. The researcher's feelings of self-doubt, uncertainty and frustration, at this stage, are well summarised by Hughes (1960), an experienced ethnographer, when he confessed that, 'I have usually been hesitant in entering the field myself and have perhaps walked around the block getting up my courage to knock at doors more often than almost any of my students' (cited in Shaffir et al., 1980, p. 28).

Despite the crucial significance of the process of negotiating entry, for without entry no ethnographic work can proceed, it has not always been awarded the attention it deserves by sociologists of education. Acknowledging the complexities, both psychological and emotional, of gaining entry, requires the production of reflexive accounts of this vital phase in the research process. Notwithstanding repeated calls for reflexivity in research reports (Hammersley, 1984) reflexive accounts of negotiating entry are rather thin on the ground. This neglect can probably be accounted for by researcher elation at finally gaining entry, quickly giving way under pressures of data collection and analysis once the field is entered (Shaffir et al., 1980). Thus the entry phase assumes reduced significance. Another possibility, of course, is that the absence of rich and lengthy methodological accounts in many published qualitative studies is owing to publisher editing, as their priorities lie with book length and potential readership rather than with methodological development.

Those accounts which deal (but not always at length) with gaining entry and its importance in the whole research process focus on the researcher's self and the psychological difficulties and dangers the researcher encounters when negotiating with gatekeepers (Habenstein, 1970; Denzin, 1978; Shaffir et al., 1980; Hammersley and Atkinson, 1983; Benyon, 1983; Burgess, 1984; Woods, 1986; Ball, 1990a: Shaffir and Stebbins, 1991). This concentration on the self is quite proper, for successful negotiation of entry does undoubtedly require particular skills in the researcher. In order to gain entry the researcher must among many things be able to successfully 'sell' their research topic, to be aware of and use presentation of self and impression management (see, for example, Delamont (1984) on the researcher's use of appropriate dress at the entry and access stages in schools; alternatively Parry's (1987) abandonment of clothes for access to a nudist club), to be as theoretically well prepared as possible and to know something about the research setting.

Glazer (1972), too, stresses the importance of the researcher's self, and:

> suggests that a fuller understanding of how the researcher gains
> initial acceptance is related to three components of the research
> relationship: (1) the appropriateness of the research project to the
> setting; (2) the researcher's personal makeup and his or her ability to
> enlist the support of others; and (3) the way respondents, given their
> personal needs and perspectives, view the project and the researcher.
> (cited in Shaffir et al., 1980, p. 29)

Glazer and other writers who concentrate on the importance of the self and researcher knowledge of the micro-context and the researcher's capacity to, in a sense, manipulate relationships in a micro-context, are quite correct to maintain this emphasis. The stress on self, context, meaning and understanding also resonates with a main theoretical perspective of ethnographic work, symbolic interactionism. As Shaffir and Stebbins (1991) point out:

> This emphasis suggests that entering the field and cultivating rich
> relationships are attributable mainly to the researcher's personal
> attributes and self-presentation and to others' judgements of him or her
> as a human being.   (Shaffir and Stebbins, 1991, p. 29)

However, I want to suggest in this chapter that by solely concentrating on researcher's self and micro-context as explanatory factors in the successful, or indeed unsuccessful, negotiation of entry in research projects, methodological writers obscure the influence of the macro-context on research relationships. This difficulty is, of course, a form of the micro-macro problem (Hargreaves, 1986). What are the relative influences of the micro and macro on the meanings and actions of actors in particular social contexts?

I want to concentrate on and develop Glazer's third component of research relationships in the entry process, i.e. 'the way respondents, given their personal needs and perspectives view the project and the researcher'. I will do this by not focusing on the researcher's self and the micro-context in the negotiation process, but upon the macro-context in which the negotiation is occurring. I am interested here in what ways the 'needs' and 'perspectives' of participants may be influenced by forces beyond the micro-context of the school. In doing this I am not questioning the importance of self and micro-context: indeed this is certainly the basis of a further article. I feel this is not merely a theoretically and methodologically important task but it is an approach which has the capacity, in going beyond the micro, to assess the impact of wider social forces on the organisational culture of the school (Reynolds, 1984; Gillborn, 1994) and by integrating policy analysis with ethnography, provide a 'bigger picture' (Ozga, 1990) than ethnography could alone.

This change in emphasis is important because ethnographers trying to accomplish entry to schools must appreciate that they are attempting entry to a changed context. Since the introduction of the 1988 Education Reform Act schools in all sectors of the education system have been subjected to change on an unprecedented scale (Flude and Hammer, 1990). It is now timely for ethnographers to calculate the implications of these changes for their own projects.

Background to the research

In the remainder of the chapter I want to provide a macro-contextualisation of my attempts to gain entry in my present research project. It is necessary, therefore, to describe it briefly. The research took the form of the conventional stages of: the identification of a research topic; the preparation of a research proposal; the submission of the proposal to a funding body; the identification of likely settings for ethnographic fieldwork; the negotiation of entry to apparently suitable settings; the negotiation of access to participants; and the ongoing data collection, analysis and writing. The substantive focus of the research was an investigation into the impact of education reform (those measures contained within the Education Reform Act 1988) on the work of primary school teachers in the English education system. The research was conducted in one English Local Education Authority in the period 1992-1996. I intended to collect data as participant observer and using semi-structured interviews with teachers in a comparative study of two primary schools. Negotiating with a great many schools took five months and I eventually only gained entry to one school, therefore having to modify the research proposal and research plans. I subsequently spent eighteen months engaged in fieldwork in this school. The comparative approach using two schools was abandoned but a method incorporating constant comparison (Glaser and Strauss, 1967) was still possible within one school.

In the following sections I explore instances when I was not granted entry. In the article I discuss negotiations with eleven schools and the reasons for refused entry. The names of the schools are substituted by a letter of the alphabet and they are categorised as shown in table 1. In the chapter these cases will be placed in a context which goes beyond the researcher's self, research relationships and the micro-context and considers wider social forces in the macro-context of the negotiations. The section headings, therefore, represent explanatory factors for my unsuccessful attempts to gain entry. These categories overlap and interrelate they are treated separately here simply to aid analysis.

The intensification of teachers' work

Of all the recent changes which have taken place in teachers' work perhaps the most striking and well-documented change is in the amount of work itself and the time expended in doing it (Apple, 1986: Campbell et al., 1993; Pollard et al., 1994; Woods, 1994a: Hargreaves, 1994). In teachers' work more and more has to be done as the pace of curriculum reform has accelerated since the legislated changes of the Education Reform Act 1988. While the volume of work has expanded dramatically the time taken to do it has remained constant (i.e. the length of the school day). Teachers have responded to this situation either by taking short-cuts or, in the main, extending hours of work beyond the school day leading to the erosion of leisure and relaxation time (Hargreaves, 1994).

One headteacher with whom I was negotiating entry spoke of the tiredness of the staff and mentioned that a husband of one of the teachers had telephoned him to complain that his wife worked at home every night until 9 o'clock on school work and was there anything the headteacher could do about this (School A). A major aspect of the pace and orchestration of change, involving further work, has been the frequency of policy documents which arrived regularly at schools from central agencies such as the National Curriculum Council and the School Examinations and Assessment Council (recently amalgamated into the School Curriculum and Assessment Authority). Schools have been charged with the implementation of these policy documents, they are Statutory Orders not merely educational advice. This has been no straightforward matter as not only have teachers had to cope with the sheer volume of policy paperwork but also to accommodate to the many changes which have taken place in policy since 1988. Frequent curricular and assessment reviews have meant that the teachers have had considerably more work to do in implementation and they have had to do this in a constantly changing context, one characterised by ambiguity, uncertainty and insecurity.

Schools have responded differently to this policy onslaught. While some schools with a history of professional self-confidence and innovation have taken ownership of the documents, 'decoded them' and used them to the school's ends, others less professionally confident and unused to change have been swamped by the documentation, and in awe of the authority of it, have slavishly tried to implement policy to the letter (Bowe and Ball, 1992). The latter adaptation has proved unproductive for many as it does not take account of either the contradictions built into policy (some aspects may be impossible to implement by anybody) or the rapidly changing nature of the policy following frequent review. Some primary headteachers who have recognised that their staffs have been fully stretched in implementing existing policy have been reluctant to burden their teachers further by giving them access to new or amended policies. This has literally meant that the heads shielded and protected their staffs by not informing them of current changes or upcoming changes, for it would further dispirit them and devalue their existing efforts at implementation. This, of course, has implications for the culture of the school. One headteacher with whom I was negotiating entry claimed that his school had developed a 'siege mentality' (Woods, 1994a):

> To survive the past four years staff had to rely on mutual support, this leads to insularity. The head deals with outside agencies. As head I deal with all outside agencies to prevent overload and staff worrying, I try to shield the staff. (Headteacher, School A)

Now, as a researcher approaching the school I was of course, in the perspective of the headteacher, merely another outside agency to protect his staff from. Since my research required teachers in the school to divert time and energy to my research enterprise and, for all they knew, subject their practice to critical scrutiny, it was not surprising that this headteacher, perhaps fearing my presence would increase work levels for his staff, did not grant entry. On several occasions heads, who had been enthusiastic about my research in the negotiation stage, told me that they would put my request to the Senior Management Team (SMT) and if they agreed then permission to research would be granted. Many of these apparently enthusiastic heads phoned back to say they had done this but their SMT had been unwilling to have me in the school. Given the strength of the 'siege mentality' in many schools and the adaptation of headteachers to protect their staffs, I conjectured how many headteachers actually did go through this process. Heads wanting to shield staff would presumably not tell the SMT, and when they phoned me back they could then deny entry but continue to proclaim their enthusiasm for the project whilst laying off responsibility for the refusal on to the SMT, a body, of course, whom in these circumstances I had not been given the opportunity to meet. Alternatively, the headteacher's enthusiasm may have been generated by actually meeting the researcher. Where the SMT have not had the same experience they may be suspicious of the researcher and have anxieties concerning the research process which the researcher has no opportunity of diffusing.

From my theoretical preparation it was evident to me that the intensification of work would be a key category to be explored. It was, therefore, the ultimate in irony to be denied access to schools when the stated reason was work overload of teachers and the pace of educational change, the very things I wished to research. Irony is also a salient feature of the categories which follow.

Fear of surveillance from external 'experts'

Primary teachers no longer work in isolation, with measures such as teacher appraisal, including classroom observation and the requirement of curriculum coordinators having to spread good practice throughout the school by working alongside colleagues. Despite the move to collaborative working as a new occupational culture which is now becoming almost mandatory (Lawn, 1988), many schools still maintain an 'old' occupational culture characterised by teachers working in isolation from their colleagues. In this type of culture the 'walls of privatism' (Fullan, 1988) remain uncracked. It is a culture of individualism and privatism in which working collaboratively and engaging in shared professional learning (Nias et al., 1992) does not occur. In a culture of individualism and privatism teachers may come to fear observation of their work by colleagues. This fear would probably be greater if external authorities were involved, for example, local authority advisers/inspectors or Office for Standards in Education (Ofsted) inspectors.

Some schools, in addition to developing the 'siege mentality', have experienced the 'Key Stage Cops' syndrome (Campbell et al., 1992). In this condition teachers perceive that the National Curriculum has been devised by external 'experts' and then handed down to the teachers for implementation. This is a centre-periphery model of curriculum development. Because of the complexity, and in some senses novelty, of the National Curriculum, the teachers come to experience feelings of inadequacy as they wonder if they are implementing the reforms in the exact ways that the external 'experts' intended. As they struggle to implement the curriculum they also know that 'policing' systems are in place to ensure that they plan, teach and assess in line with the National Curriculum requirements. In the 'Key Stage Cops' syndrome feelings of inadequacy coupled with knowledge of accountability systems, and knowledge that they are accountable to a large range of constituencies, results in fear of surveillance of their work by outside 'experts'. The teachers are constantly looking over their shoulders and feeling that they may be doing things wrongly and that at any moment somebody is going to discover this, with dire consequences for the teacher. Campbell et al. (1992) describe this as a 'paranoia about accountability' with teachers living in fear of 'the Key Stage Cops' coming. However, 'it was a figment of the imagination, given the numbers of inspectors in relation to schools, but (nevertheless) was a real influence on the way teachers saw their work' (p. 8).

The director of the National Primary Centre in the region in which I was negotiating entry with schools considered that this atmosphere of fear would actually increase my chances of gaining entry, since heads were looking for ways to get teachers into the classrooms of their colleagues to 'get them used to observation and having someone in the room in a non-threatening way before the men (sic) with clipboards arrive'. He thought that the presence of a researcher would serve the same function. However, in one school in which the staff were used to working co-operatively (school A) the threat of external surveillance from an unknown outsider, the researcher, was too much to allow entry. The headteacher of this school put my research proposal to his staff, at a full staff meeting, and reported back to me that;

> Five years ago you wouldn't have had this problem. I was quite amazed at the reactions of the staff and they are used to working collaboratively with each other and alongside advisers and advisory teachers, classroom observation seems to be the sticking point. One teacher had said at the staff meeting 'the thought of being observed makes me feel all funny inside'.   (Headteacher, School A)

This mode of adaptation could be considered as a manifestation of deskilling as some teachers come to lose ownership of their traditional craft skills as their work becomes merely to implement the plans devised by others, elsewhere. Kincheloe (1991) has argued that in advanced capitalist societies conceptions of scientific technical rationality are dominant and the prevailing conception of science is one of positivism. In this 'culture of positivism' (Giroux, 1981, following Horkheimer, 1974), the 'expert' comes to oppress the non-experts, who see the judgement of the oppressive expert and the system in which it is made as legitimate (Marcuse, 1964). In this way the oppressed contribute to their own oppression. In the 'Key Stage Cops' syndrome the teachers come to fear further oppression from external experts.

At one school (School B) negotiation of entry was postponed by the female headteacher because the school was shortly to have its first Ofsted general inspection. After the inspection the headteacher merely telephoned to tell me that there was no point in visiting the school to negotiate. Others with close connections with the school, an education lecturer and researcher who was liaison tutor for the school and a teacher who was a parent of a child at the school, later told me that the inspectors had been highly critical of the school in their published report. During the inspection the inspectors had been openly critical of the teachers' practice and had communicated this in a rude and unprofessional way. This news had reverberated around the other schools in the district and fuelled the fear of external surveillance. This may be the intention behind government policy on school improvement, for following news of the first primary school to fail inspection on 3 November 1993, John Patten, the then Secretary of State for Education, 'was careful to stress that most schools in Britain did a terrific job. He said "there are schools which sometimes do badly ... small handful but let's hope the mere fact of publication will spur on all schools that might fall under this particular glare"' (*The Guardian*, 4 November 1993). These events were occurring at the time of my entry negotiations.

Teacher perceptions of educational researchers

Historically teachers and educational researchers have not enjoyed good relations. The findings of sociologists have proved, in the past, to be largely irrelevant to life in schools and teachers' daily concerns. In other words, 'sociologists' typical theoretical abstraction seemed remote from the hard realism of the school' (Woods and Pollard, 1988, p. 8). Another factor which may worsen relations between teachers and researchers is that the teachers may come to feel that they are merely being 'used' by the researcher. As one researcher (Beynon, 1983, p. 47) was told, 'When you first arrived we all thought here's another bloke getting a degree on our backs! We resented the idea we were just fodder for research'. Teachers have also not fared well from some of the findings of educational researchers, for since the late 1960s the practice of 'teacher bashing' has been as prevalent amongst sociologists as it has been amongst members of the Right. Extreme right wing politicians and party advisers 'bashed' teachers (at length in the media) because they were held to be 'trendy', left-wing subversives who were undermining the educational standards of the children they taught (or more correctly from their perspective didn't teach) and were destroying the moral character of a once-great nation.

For some sociologists of education, particularly neo-Marxists, teachers were seen to be witting or unwitting agents of the state, which in capitalist societies preserved the conditions for capital to flourish. The role that teachers were held to play in this type of society was in the maintenance of the *status quo*, sustaining the unjust society and the reproduction of the next labour force by equipping them with the correct dispositions and skills (with an emphasis on dispositions) with which to generate surplus value for capital. Teachers in this view were mere servants of the state (Lawn and Grace, 1987). Teachers are, I believe, still reeling from the blows which they have received from both the Left and the Right. Bashing has not been limited to teachers, however. As early as the 1950s David Eccles, the Tory Minister of Education (and *ex officio* president of the National Foundation of Educational Research!), declared that 'educational research was an activity imposed by the long haired on the long suffering' (cited in Cunningham, 1988, p. 44). This relatively humorous abuse has recently grown more serious. Sociologists and social scientists have in turn been bashed by the New Right and subjected to a similarly vehement 'discourse of derision' (Ball, 1990b) as the teachers. This has resulted in, for example, a movement away from theoretically-based courses in higher education (including, of course, sociology of education for intending teachers) towards the practice-oriented, school-based preparation of teachers. Educational research findings have been subject to abuse and misuse by central government, and policy-making has not been informed by research (except a particular kind see Alexander et al., 1992, and Hammersley and Scarth's 1993 critique) but by dogma forged in a climate of non-rationality (Gipps, 1993; Black, 1993).

The alleged irrelevance of research, and the public rubbishing of researchers and their research products might lie behind the comment of one headteacher who replied to my request for entry that he thought 'research (including my proposed research) was saturated with aspects not related to real learning for the children' (School C). This quotation also reveals a recognition that not only might schools consider educational research irrelevant to educational practice but accurately, that until recently (Pollard, 1990; Woods, 1993) sociologists have eschewed topics related directly to teaching and learning.

The presence of other researchers

The teacher as researcher (Stenhouse, 1975) and reflective pedagogy movements have now become the new orthodoxies of initial teacher education (Menter and Pollard, 1989). In these models of teacher preparation and professional development the traditional barriers lying between theory, research and practice are broken down as practitioners themselves engage in research on their own practice (and perhaps the practice of colleagues) which involves the stages of issue identification, data collecting, analysis and reflection informing the next phase in a spiralling programme of action and reflection (Pollard and Tann, 1987). These pedagogic philosophies articulate well with school-based models of teacher education because, being implemented in the workplace, they legitimate practitioner knowledge and encourage both practical theorising and the theorisation of practice. Courses in initial teacher education now typically involve forms of serial and block school experience which involve students in not only learning practical aspects of teaching but in research and reflection on that teaching and the context in which it takes place. Course requirements in initial teacher education often include the assessment of small-scale. practice-oriented research conducted by students. These requirements place an additional responsibility on the schools because they are now required to accept students for the traditional 'teaching practice' elements of courses and also accept students for research projects. Many of the schools I contacted in initial negotiations refused at an early stage because they claimed to have students already in school conducting research.

Courses for practising teachers, too, are influenced strongly by notions of practitioner research and reflective teaching, sometimes expressed in the notion of action research. Owing to the demise of long award-bearing courses involving teacher secondments, teachers are increasingly engaging in professional development in the workplace on a part-time basis and often financed by the teachers themselves. These changes stimulated by Local Management of Schools, including formula funding, have ensured that teacher research is often confined to the teacher's workplace. Several schools I approached (Schools C, D, F, G, H) said that their school 'had been researched', or was being researched 'by a teacher at the school', and that 'it would be unwise for me to carry out further research at their school' (School C).

The area in which I was intending to undertake the research was one in which there were several institutions of higher education. Each of these institutions had departments of education. Particular schools, therefore, were either consistently approached by postgraduate research students or had postgraduates already in the school.

A philosophy of vocational preparation and development which stresses the centrality of the research process in practitioner learning is not restricted to teacher education but also underpins other types of post-16 education. In further education, courses such as Business and Technician Education Council (BTEC), National Vocational Qualifications (NVQ) in the 'caring' semi-professions such as nursery nursing, often include a school-based placement in which small-scale research or the production of a report of the placement is a course requirement. Even students at secondary schools taking Technical and Vocational Educational Initiative (TVEI) courses or on work experience courses may be required to complete an information-gathering exercise and a report to satisfy course assessment criteria. Many of the schools where I failed to gain entry stated that they had a number of students from higher and further education already in the school and that this was adding to the workload of the staff. Approaches to local authority advisory staff to ask them to suggest suitable schools for the research to take place often resulted in the staff recommending the same small handful of schools, which consequently were presumably inundated by many interested researchers.

Entry was denied to me on some occasions owing to the headteacher having perceived the behaviour of a previous researcher as unethical or insensitive. For instance, some schools mentioned that they had had a researcher previously who had been 'very critical of the school' and who had not 'handled the feedback session with staff very well' (School H). Comments such as these elicited recollections of documented reflexive accounts of the dissemination of research reports by the researcher to the researched (Ball, 1984; Woods, 1994b), a process which is difficult for the researcher to control. It is difficult to stop implied criticism from being personalised, and easy to fall foul of the micro-politics of the institution as warring factions amongst the researched turn researchers' findings to their own purposes, to gain political advantage. It is a process, too, in which the researched may come to avoid the gaze of researchers in future and thus avoid any actual or implied criticism, which may come from the findings of a researcher working in a 'critical' tradition. Obviously trying to gain entry to a school where another researcher has 'queered the pitch' is fraught with problems, even if entry is gained in such circumstances subsequent attempts to negotiate access to participants would probably be unfruitful. Once bitten, as they say, is twice shy.

Changing patterns of teacher education

The Tory government's fear of the radical and subversive potential of educational theory (Dale, 1992), linked with a desire to reduce public expenditure, introduced school-based patterns of teacher training. The reduction/exclusion of theory which is 'delivered' in higher education institutions has meant that more and more students are spending more and more time in schools on serial and block school experience. The amount of time that BEd and postgraduate certificate in education (PGCE) students have to spend in schools has increased steadily since 1988, while academic preparation for teaching has been confined largely to subject specialist studies of National Curriculum subjects. These changes have made increased demands on schools to accept more students more often and develop systems such as mentoring schemes to facilitate the school-based training.

At one large primary school (School H, 450 pupils) I negotiated with, attempting to gain entry involved me in talks with the headteacher and being given the opportunity to 'sell' my research to the Senior Management Team. At the end of my talk I invited questions from the staff who were present. The deputy headteacher, who was also responsible for student teachers in the school, said that my research was out of the question. This was because each term they had large groups of students in school. The next term, the term I envisaged starting my research, they had twenty-two students for five weeks. With almost every teacher responsible for one or more students in their classes, the deputy thought it unrealistic that the school could also cope with a researcher, who, like the students, would also place demands of lesson observation and talking to (interviewing) teachers, on to the school.

The declining powers of local education authorities

Since 1979 there have been repeated policy initiatives which, while paradoxically strengthening and increasing powers of central government, have reduced the power and authority of local government. In the domain of education this diminution of local authority control has taken many different forms. Local education authorities (LEAs) are now significantly less influential in the running of schools. Financial control has been been devolved to headteachers and governors. The changed power relationships have produced a new culture in which local authority advisers and administrators, rather than controlling budgets and making allocations to schools, compete with other 'providers' in supplying services to the schools. Some of these local authority officials, particularly in LEAs which prior to 1988 had adopted a bureaucratic, authoritarian and top-down approach to their schools, are now, to borrow the words of one headteacher, 'yesterday's men' (sic) (School E).

The changed culture and shift of power have significance for the researcher wishing to negotiate entry to schools. In the past it was not uncommon for researchers to request entry to a local authority school by directing the request to the Chief Education Officer (CEO) (see for example, Hammersley, 1984) or LEA adviser. The researcher in these circumstances was granted entry to a potentially suitable setting(s) on the strength of a headteacher receiving a letter from the CEO. With the recent changes this strategy is becoming increasingly difficult. While anticipating the situation and not approaching the CEO, I did contact two LEA advisers (recently redesignated as inspectors) to ask if they could give me the names of schools in their areas which conformed to the criteria I had in mind (numbers of children, staff, location etc.). The LEA inspectors did give me names of schools I could negotiate with but were reluctant to contact the schools on my behalf or to send a letter of introduction or recommendation. This could represent an acknowledgement of their reduced power and influence with the school and headteachers. They could no longer make demands on schools. From my perspective I was pleased that in my negotiations with schools I would not appear to be associated with the local inspectors because in their new inspectorial role as Ofsted registered inspectors (inspecting schools in other divisions of the authority, inspecting schools in their own area being proscribed), they of course constituted agents of external surveillance, a role as researcher (seeking entry and later access) I did not wish to adopt by association.

Financial considerations

With the introduction of the market philosophy into education schools have changed dramatically as organisational cultures (Bowe and Ball, 1992). Schools must now consider aspects of management which prior to 1988 would be considered only applicable to the industrial and commercial sectors. With delegated budgets and local financial management has come the behaviour and discourse of the market-place. Large primary schools now have a bursar or financial officer on the payroll (Mortimore et al., 1994) and headteachers of large primaries are being drawn into financial management and away from professional curriculum leadership (Ball, 1988; Hellawell, 1990; Bowe and Ball, 1992; Pollard et al., 1994; Troman, 1994). With these changes primary schools now deal routinely with the financial considerations of budgeting, financial planning, auditing, marketing, calculations of effectiveness and efficiency and cost-benefit analyses. As it is a requirement of four yearly Ofsted inspection that each primary school should demonstrate how its financial management articulates with curriculum management, the production of school development plans has become a necessary as well as legal requirement. Financial procedures such as these have forced schools to consider aspects of school life which perhaps were not considered previously, particularly so when coupled with other features of the reforms. For example, now that the initial training of teachers is more school-based and schools submit costed bids for training students, it has become necessary for schools to be able to put a cost on teachers' time, if they are to act as mentors, in order to calculate the costs and benefits of the school taking on a commitment to training students. With this commodification of teachers it is entirely possible (some would say reasonable) for the school to charge the researcher for the teacher's time or the cost of a supply teacher in order to release a teacher, during the school day, to be interviewed by a researcher. One headteacher (School J) referred to this as the researcher getting 'quality time' (i.e. free of interruption and not at the end of a busy teaching day) and of course, 'quality time isn't cheap'.

It is, of course, important that the school continues to attract sufficient age-weighted pupil units (children) each one carrying a fixed amount of money according to age and at the end of the school year the books balance and the school avoids financial loss. These financial procedures, market principles and an atmosphere in which schools perhaps do not seek to make a profit but try to avoid losses, create a culture in which social relations become mediated by the cash nexus. This has implications for research and especially for the negotiation of entry. No headteacher with whom I negotiated requested that I pay the school a fee in return for researching the school. This, however, has been the experience of other researchers (Rudduck and Nixon, 1992). I did feel, however, in some circumstances, if I had offered money entry might have been granted. If schools are going to divert teacher time and resources to assisting researchers in their projects I suspect schools, in the type of financial climate I have described, will become increasingly reluctant to involve themselves in research. Hitherto, educational researchers have always had to rely on the goodwill of teachers in order to research schools. Even so, the research process, including gaining entry, was never free of ethical issues and considerations. Paying for entry might not only materially change the relationships between the researcher, gatekeeper and participants, it might also raise a new agenda of issues in the ethics of ethnography!

Headteacher illness, burn-out and envy

In many schools it is the headteacher who has borne the brunt of many of the recent changes. It is the headteacher who has shielded and protected the staff from the policy onslaught and frequent changes in policy and external agencies; experienced strategic compliance as they have been forced to conceal personal and collective educational values and adopt imposed ones; experienced role conflict and ambiguity as they tried to fulfil chief executive and leading professional roles (Hughes, 1985); been responsible for balancing the books; constantly worried about the efficacy of marketing strategies; in some schools managed change unsupported by a hostile governing body; been largely responsible for unfavourable inspection reports; and in most of these situations coped alone and in isolation from their governors and staffs (*Times Educational Supplement,* 28 October 1994, p. 15).

Such conditions have, however, created casualties. The number of teachers and headteachers who have retired early or are seeking early retirement through ill health has increased alarmingly since 1988 (McCleod and Meikle, 1994). As headteachers are the likely gatekeeper that the researcher will encounter, headteacher stress, illness and burn-out may impact on negotiating entry. In the stage of my research when I was trying to identify a sample of suitable schools to approach, I asked an education lecturer in a local college who had considerable experience of local schools if she could recommend some for me to approach. Before making her recommendations she spent quite a time explaining the difficulties in approaching schools in her area owing to headteacher long-term sickness, breakdown or because a headteacher was so stressed it was causing difficulties in staff relationships and morale in schools. I had already had experience of this in my 'uninformed' approaches to school. At one school, although the headteacher was present in school he clearly was not well and the deputy was effectively the headteacher. In this case the headteacher (who had been apparently very enthusiastic in his dealings with me) refused entry because of what he described as a 'political' situation in the school (School H). At another school (School E) I was negotiating with a headteacher who spent the whole of the interview slumped in his executive chair with his head rested on one hand staring at his desk. He was half turned away from me and not establishing eye contact or speaking. After fifteen minutes he suddenly broke down and explained to me that the evening before he had resigned at a governor's meeting and would be leaving at the end of term, and thought that in these circumstances the school would be unsuitable for my research.

Opportunities for teachers and headteachers to escape, albeit briefly, from the relentless pace and pressure of change are decreasing. The much-needed space, away from the workplace, in which to recharge professional and personal batteries, catch up on one's subject, engage in reflection and renew commitment to the profession is no longer available to many teachers and headteachers (Hargreaves, 1994). Secondment and full-time award-bearing courses, which so often served these purposes in the past, are no longer available in the changed financial climate and currently dominant views concerning professional development (i.e. it should be school-based and directly linked to school concerns). Non-stipendiary teacher fellowships, too, which offer a much-needed space for professional development away from the chalk face, although still available, are receiving fewer and fewer applications as schools become reluctant to sacrifice a member of staff for one term and incur the additional financial burden of paying a supply teacher's salary (*The Guardian*, 4 October 1994).

By comparison the researcher receiving a research award for a three year funded research project has the opportunity to follow their own research interests, have time for critical reflection, and all the advantages which are denied to the full-time teacher and headteacher. The headteacher who broke down during interview (School E) considered being paid to do research for three years was a 'luxury' and something he wished he had the opportunity to do (he said this with a cynical tone). This perception is supported by the reaction of a deputy headteacher of an inner-city school in which I had previously worked as a supply teacher. When I told him I was unavailable for supply work because I was now undertaking educational research full-time, he replied (in a sarcastic tone) '... well I suppose it's more relaxing than coming here and teaching our kids'. I know from experience that research is no rest cure but from the teacher and headteacher perspective it may be seen as an attractive alternative, a 'luxury' form of escape from the daily routine and rigours of the classroom and school. Thus, headteacher envy of the researcher seemed yet another factor to consider in the gaining entry process.

The temporal phenomenology of the school

Stephen Ball (1983) has pointed out that as far as he is aware in existing case-studies of the school, 'the nature of social life is assumed to be unaffected by the point of the cycle at which the fieldwork occurs' (p. 81). This would seem to be a rather serious neglect by sociologists of education. For even at a common-sense level the time of year a study is conducted would probably affect not only the type of data available but also the availability of participants to provide data. It is well known, for example, that the autumn term, which concludes in December with Christmas celebrations, is a notoriously busy term for the primary school. Indeed, prior to negotiating with School K, a primary school adviser warned me half-way through November that I would be wasting my time negotiating entry at this stage in the school year because 'Mary and Joseph will be well out of the stock cupboards by now'. Teachers who are faced with the implementation of the National Curriculum and the extra-curricular events traditionally arising at Christmas would have little time to devote to an ethnographer keen to engage in observation, formal and informal interviewing.

School philosophies regarding the educational visits of children and the timing of these visits can also affect entry negotiations. One headteacher (School I) in a written communication with me felt that, 'we are unable to help you with your research next term. We have many events and happenings during this time, with two classes at college and others on a residential visit, that I feel you would not get the continuity you need'. It is likely that the timing of traditional events and school visits, which occur in some terms more than others, have always affected entry negotiations. However, the recent changes regarding assessment and testing in the National Curriculum have compounded these difficulties.

The requirement that schools carry out Standard Assessment Tasks (SATs) with children in Year 2 at the end of Key Stage I and with Year 6 at the end of Key Stage 2 has made significant time demands on primary schools during the spring and summer terms. Large class sizes plus the direction that the teachers conduct individual and small group tests (e.g. the Key Stage I Reading Test) has meant that schools have had to devise strategies to support teachers who are administering the tests. It is common, for instance, at Key Stage I for the school to hire a supply teacher to teach the class while the regular class teacher withdraws groups for testing. Alternatively, learning support assistants are deployed to occupy and contain a class with 'holding activities' while the teacher conducts the individual or group tests. In some schools (usually the larger primaries) the normally non-teaching headteacher will take the majority of the class or classes for an activity away from the classroom (games and country dancing are popular) while the teachers carry out the tests with groups. In some schools children not being tested in a particular class are split up and join other teachers with their classes for the duration of the group test. Withdrawal of children, for testing, from whole school activities (for example assemblies), allows staff to colonise time not usually their own.

While testing is taking place key personnel are also involved out of school time in the marking, moderation, recording and reporting of pupil achievement. This adds to the intensification of their work and of course makes them unavailable to the researcher during this part of the yearly cycle. In School H, when negotiating entry with the SMT, it was, I believe, the reaction of the headteacher of infants (the department most affected by national testing) to my research proposal which was instrumental in preventing me from gaining entry. When asked directly by the deputy headteacher if she would mind me being present when the SATs were being carried out, she said she definitely would and she thought research under these circumstances would be unthinkable. The tests, although taken by one age group in each Key Stage, can, in one way or another, involve nearly the whole school. They affect negotiation of entry, for headteachers readily anticipate the problems associated with these phases in the temporal cycle of the school year and do not welcome adding to them by inviting the presence of an ethnographic fieldworker.

Conclusion

This chapter, in focusing on the macro-context of the research experience of unsuccessful attempts to negotiate entry, has attempted to rationalise failure. At the same time it has avoided too much of the self-doubt and anxiety (although these were felt acutely while engaged in the process of gaining entry) typical of those accounts which reflect solely on the significance of the researcher's self. Although acknowledging the importance of researcher's self, research relations and the micro-context, the focus throughout the article has been on the impact of wider social forces on both educational change and entry negotiations. I have identified twelve interrelated explanatory factors which seemed to be involved in gatekeeper decisions not to grant me entry to educational settings.

Three further lessons can be gleaned from these fieldwork experiences. First, the collection, analysis and contextualisation of data in all phases of research, in the case of this research the gaining entry phase, facilitates the production of reflexive accounts. Reflexivity not only contributes rigour to the ethnographic process but is also a prerequisite for the generation of theory. The macro-theorisation of my unsuccessful attempts eventually enabled me to devise strategies which ensured successful entry.

Secondly, I am not trying to suggest, by concentrating on structure and macro-context, that gaining entry is an 'overdetermined' process. Researcher self, agency and micro-context still remain as vital factors in the successful negotiation of entry. I am suggesting, however, that researchers, at least in the context of the English education system, will need to pay attention to the wider context, (e.g. political, ideological, policy contexts), in their negotiations with educational gatekeepers. This is necessary because researchers, intent on producing school ethnographies, are entering a rapidly changing scene and the impetus for change is largely external to the school. Participants wearied by change are increasingly resistant to the academic researcher. The days are gone when the researcher could effortlessly enter the field, as Erickson (1986) notes, in opposition, 'with only a *tabula rasa* mind carrying only a toothbrush and a hunting knife' (p. 140). Or to put it another way, getting in is getting harder.

Thirdly and finally, the fieldwork research experiences reported in this chapter have raised a general question about teachers and researchers and the relationship between them. Theorising from the data and experiences of not gaining entry leads me to conjecture that the reluctance of schools to collaborate with an academic ethnographic researcher could be a yet further indication of the increasing technification of teaching (Apple, 1986). This situation is unfortunate in the extreme for it coincides with a time when researchers working in the critical ethnographic tradition are only just beginning to develop and support collaborative forms of 'educative' research involving coalitions of teachers and researchers (Gitlin et al., 1992; Woods and Wenham, 1994). Headteachers and teachers, deskilled in the sense that they no longer engage in critical reflection on the very measures which disempower them, are the ones most likely to exhibit no entry signs when engaged in negotiations with ethnographers.

Notes

Table I. Reasons for refused entry

Reasons for refused entry	School
The intensification of teachers' work	A,D,E,F,H
Fear of surveillance from external experts	A.B
Teachers' perceptions of educational researchers	C
The presence of other researchers	C,D,F,G,H
Changing patterns of teacher education	H.I
The declining powers of local education authorities	E
Financial considerations	J
Headteacher illness, burn-out, envy	E,H
The temporal phenomenology of the school	I,K

Chapter 2

Time for ethnography

Bob Jeffrey and Geoff Troman

Fieldwork takes time. Does that make time the critical attribute of
fieldwork? According to ethnographic tradition, the answer is yes.
(Wolcott, 1995 p.77)

Introduction

Since the early days of its application, classical ethnographic research has proved
remarkably popular and successful in developing understanding of social and
cultural processes in educational settings. It has: facilitated the generation,
testing and development of differentiation-polarisation theory (Lacey, 1970;
Hargreaves, 1967; Ball, 1981); contributed in a major way to our understanding
of teacher and pupil perspectives and social processes in primary (Pollard,
1985) and secondary school (Woods, 1979; Ball, 1981); developed social
reproduction theory in studies of working class (Willis, 1977) and middle class
(Ball, 2003) pupils; illuminated how the intersections of class, ethnicity, gender
and sexuality shape student educational experience and achievement (Mac an
Ghaill, 1988); led to the generation and development of sociological theories
of educational identity and learning (Filer and Pollard, 2000); and theorised
policy process as well as demonstrating the impact of educational reform and
policies of marketisation on teachers, pupils and parents (Ball, 2003; Gewirtz,
et al., 1995; Reay, 1998).

All of these influential educational studies, employing the anthropological
method of ethnography, required researchers to invest considerable amounts
of time in fieldwork. However, an ideal length of time to be spent in the field is
difficult to establish. Wolcott (1995. p. 77), describes an ideal fieldwork term
of two years as having become the standard as 'perhaps related to the success
of Malinowski's inadvertently long fieldwork among the Trobrianders' (he had
to sit out World War I because of his Polish ancestry). Earlier anthropologists
researching rural cultures had an ideal of twelve months minimum in order to
study the annual cycle of the growing season'. Walford (2002, p. 1) argues that
the issue of time in ethnography makes long-term engagement in research sites

an activity which may be more suited to research students than it is to tenured academics:

One of the odd aspects of doing a doctorate through educational ethnography is that the chances are that, even if the successful doctoral candidate obtains a job in higher education, it is unlikely that she or he will ever conduct a full ethnographic study again. The main reason for this is, of course, that it is unlikely that there will ever be sufficient time in any academic's life to spend the year or so that is really necessary to generate data for another ethnography. It is only during the three (or more) years of doctoral research that most people have any chance of being able to free themselves from most other work commitments for the necessary period. This means that most of our 'classic' ethnographies were originally conducted as doctorates. From the early studies of Hargreaves (1967) and Lacey (1970) through to the work of Ball (1981), Burgess (1983), Aggleton (1987) and Carspecken (1991), all were originally doctoral studies.

The classic ethnographies of the Chicago tradition of the 1920s and 1930s; what Woods (1996 p.32) refers to as the 'main line' of interactionist ethnography derives from Mead, Blumer, Becker and Glaser and Strauss. If we are to understand the complexities of what is happening in social situations we need to employ an ethnographic approach, which 'captures and records the voices of lived experience ... contextualises experience ... goes beyond mere fact and surface appearances ... presents details, context, emotion, and the webs of social relationships that join persons to one another' (Denzin, 1994, p. 83).

This empirical social world is

the minute by minute, day to day social life of individuals as they interact together, as they develop understandings and meanings, as they engage in joint action and respond to each other as they adapt to situations, and as they encounter and move to resolve problems that arise through their circumstances.

(Woods 1996, p.37)

The study of the that empirical world focuses on

how understandings are formed, how meanings are negotiated, how roles are developed, how a curriculum works out, how a policy is formulated and implemented, how a pupil becomes deviant. These are processual matters, not products. Social life is ongoing, developing, fluctuating, becoming. It never arrives or ends. Some forms of behaviour may be fairly stable, others variable, others emergent. Some forms of interaction proceed in stages or phases. This again emphasises the need for long and sustained researcher immersion in the field in order to cover whole processes and produce 'thick description' (Geertz, 1973) that will encompass this richness. Processes, for example, of cultural induction, labelling, identity formation, differentiation and polarisation, curriculum modification, friendship formation—all require lengthy involvement in the research field, otherwise only part of the process will be sampled, leading to misleading analyses.   (Woods, forthcoming, p. 5)

Data, for educational research needs to be collected within the school context, since these processes are strongly shaped by that context (Rosenholtz, 1989). The major considerations for sampling, following this approach, are considered to be people, contexts and time, (Ball 1990; Hammersley and Atkinson 1995; Woods 1996).

However, the intensification of academic life (Green and Miller, 1999) and the pressures from funding bodies for quick completion make a sustained twelve month minimum research period a luxury. Most often contemporary ethnographers, 'link brief visits that extend over a long period of time, so that the brevity of the periods is mollified by the effect of long-term acquaintance' (Wolcott, 1995 p. 77).

Our main research projects—creative teaching, the intensification of teachers' work, the effects of Ofsted inspections on primary teachers and teachers' experience of stress—were restricted in the same way in relation to people, context and time. For example, the creativity research rarely included conversations with school management and was limited to a sample of about twenty teachers. The research on the intensification of teachers' work used a similar sample but did not include any students' perspectives or those of governors and parents; and the stress researcher, again with about twenty in his core sample, did not speak to respondents colleagues or family as might have been expected in a classic ethnography. The creativity researcher did not inhabit the staff room regularly in contrast to the inspection and intensification research, where it was seen as a prime site, and the stress researcher did not visit any of the work sites of the core sample but interviews were often carried out in people's homes. The length of time spent on each project was similar but there were differing time features.

Our four projects were all focused on primary teachers' responses to recent educational reforms. We charted the adaptations of 'creative teachers' to the National Curriculum and other prescribed policy changes between 1992 and 1995 in eight primary schools (Woods, 1990, 1993, 1995; Woods and Jeffrey, 1996), showing teachers not merely responding to policy prescriptions but playing an active and creative role in the implementation process. Since 1995 three allied projects with 'creative schools' have taken place (Woods, 2000; Jeffrey, 2000, 2003) which focus more on the creative learning of students. More recent work on school restructuring (Troman, 1997; Woods et al., 1997) carried out between 1994 and 1996 and the impact of Ofsted (Office for Standards in Education) inspections on primary teachers (Jeffrey and Woods, 1998) carried out from 1995-9 reported a growth of constraint, intensification of work and increasing managerialism. It was clear from this research that stress was a major aspect of primary teachers' work in the mid 1990s, and we carried out further research in this area from 1997-2000, focusing on the social aspects of stress and teachers' experiences of stress, to complement quantitative and psychological studies, which form the bulk of the existing literature.

Our review of time spent in fieldwork has identified three different time modes. While other ethnographers (see those discussed above) have used the modes in similar ways, we draw here exclusively on our own research in order to exemplify that which we believe is common to many ethnographies. We conclude with a discussion of these modes and outline some strategies for using these different time modes for gaining ethnographic research funding.

Ethnographic time modes

Ethnographic projects are never finished, only left, with their accounts considered provisional and tentative (Walker, 1986). The total length of a research project may be defined by the researcher(s) themselves indicating its closure. Alternatively, some projects are developed throughout the whole of a researcher's life, an ethnography may become a long episodic narrative. Further, the 'whole project' period does not mean that researchers work on research projects full time, for they may have other work activities alongside the research. Our own four projects had similar time parameters, from two to three years, but only sixty-three per cent of the researchers' full time work was allocated to the research.

A second feature of time, alongside the total length, is the frequency with which researchers visit sites. This varies according to access limitations, project time available and the research orientation. We have identified three modes that constitute, to some extent, the nature of our ethnographic practice, 'compressed', 'selective intermittent' and 'recurrent' modes. Each has specific features that highlight different aspects of an ethnography and may well be considered different types of research although some research projects incorporate all of them.

A *compressed* time mode

In using the concept of 'compressed time mode' we are not referring to the now much discredited practice of 'blitzkrieg ethnography' (Rist, 1980). A compressed mode involves a short period of intense ethnographic research in which researchers inhabit a research site almost permanently for anything from a few days to a month. Researchers live the life of the inhabitants as far as is possible without prejudicing the research, antagonising the inhabitants or disturbing the research site itself (Woods, 1986). A researcher on a project designed to gain a whole picture of a community or institution seeks access to all the relevant places at a research site and as many people as are available. In the case of a school, the classrooms, staff rooms, meetings, the playground, assemblies, class visits, school journeys, social gatherings of parents and teachers are relevant. This type of ethnography captures the dynamics of a context, documenting the visible and less tangible social structures and relations. Observational field notes are a central part of the data as opportunities for conversations with inhabitants is often restricted for they are fully engaged with daily routines. There is a lot of hanging around, soaking up every tiny detail in case it might be of some particular significance in later analysis. The research site's routines, tensions and disturbances are all recorded (see the 'Story of an Inspection' in Jeffrey and Woods 1998).

The observation of so many contexts and interactions in the compressed mode lead to a proliferation of observations and perspectives, which need organising *in situ*. Peter Woods volunteered to join a school journey to the Isle of Wight in Southern England for a week with year six students, aged from ten to eleven years-old. The opportunity provided him with an ideal research project. His early observations and thoughts recorded in field notes, late at night in bed, included full details of every minute of his compressed task. Memos generated preliminary analysis, during quiet times, contained concepts which began to theorise the school visit. The main features identified were: *de-institutionalisation; communitas; educational activities; atmospheres; roles; rule-governed relations* (Woods 2000).

Another approach is to identify one embracing theme to determine the research focus. Geoff joined one school for a week to explore how and why the head and teachers considered it to be a 'low stress' school. In this compressed period he carried out interviews and complemented them by gathering documentation and observed staff room interactions. His focus was the distribution of power in the school past and present (Troman and Woods, 2001).

A third method of responding to the proliferation of observational data, is to make use of synecdoche—portraying a part of a picture as a representation of the whole picture—as a way of 'seeing into the life of things' (Woods, 1996, p.77). Ofsted inspectors usually descend on a school early on a Monday morning and stay until Thursday evening from seven o'clock each morning until late in the evening. They are given their own room and expect open access to all areas in the school including toilets and kitchens and to everyone who crosses the threshold of the site including parents, governors and students. However, there was one place they were not welcome and that was the staff room.

Contrary to the inspectors' authoritative freedom the researcher was only allowed access to this room during the week of the inspection. He was not allowed elsewhere in the school in case he interfered with the inspection process. Nevertheless, he had the opportunity to inhabit the place where much of the drama of the week was considered, interrogated and reviewed by teachers. He was privy to emotional reactions, moments of exhilaration and quiet brooding periods. The compact nature of the research, always in the staff room, on each day until all the staff left in the evening meant attention to the minutia of a context—changing and differing atmospheres, interactive behaviours, tensions and coping strategies. In particular it was possible to identify exhibitions of solidarity, insularity, self denigration, anger, humour, panic, resistance, empathy, support and obliviousness. The temporal/emotional phases of the inspection week—Early Encounters–Last Performance–Celebration and Review—could then be mapped out, in order to construct the 'career' of the inspection (Jeffrey and Woods 1998).

A written evocation of the observed research experience of a compressed time slot provides a representation of a larger picture constructed over longer periods. The main feature of a compressed ethnographic period is the portrayal of a snapshot in time of a particular site or event, one in which all perspectives are particularly relevant and the interaction of people and context is described in detail. It is often more context led than interview dominant and is similar to that of a critical event (Woods, 1993).

A *selective intermittent* time mode

This mode is one where the length of time spent doing the research is longer, for example: from three months to two years but with a very flexible approach to the frequency of site visits. The frequency depends on the researcher selecting particular foci as the research develops and on selecting the relevant events. The dominant criterion is depth of study, entailing progressive focusing (Strauss and Corbin, 1990) for a sustained period. Apart from the initial period of broad familiarisation, specific rich contexts are selected for examination and interpretation. There is less 'hanging around' as the research develops than there might be in a compressed approach where a continuous length of time in the field is stipulated. This type of research specifies the specific area for investigation such as a curriculum, hierarchies, gender relations, micro politics, student teacher relations but the researcher would be continually selective about the place and the people with whom they spent time.

Although the total amount of time for the research may have been designated in the research design the amount of time actually spent in fieldwork and the frequency with which researchers visit sites is not determined by the design. Time in the field is determined by decisions as to whether the analytical categories have been 'saturated' (Strauss and Corbin, 1990). There is a much more fluid relationship between the extent of fieldwork and analysis than in the other two time modes.

Our creativity and intensification research projects fitted this model. The objective of the creativity project was to record the impact of national educational reforms on primary teachers' creativity and to show their adaptations and appropriations. We needed about two terms—two-thirds of a year—to gain an adequate knowledge of the range of teaching and learning strategies used by teachers. However, the objective was not to provide a broad picture but to find out what constituted those strategies, to detail their features, to ascertain the quality of the interactions and outcomes. We took time to interpret and problematise practices that were considered routine and then discussed, reflected and reviewed them with teachers.

We also needed time to allow the relationships to develop, in order to ensure greater collaborative investigation between teacher and researcher. We needed time between visits to reflect on our observations and conversations and to experiment with relevant theories to interpret the data from the site. We then re-visited the site when we were ready to view the teachers' practices from a new perspective. Conversely, teachers informed us of relevant events and we altered plans to accommodate these specific topics:

> In Marilyn's Tudor topic, the Year 6 pupils learnt a musical, choreographed some dances, composed some Tudor music, visited Hampton Court, watched part of the film of Columbus and a TV series, read 'fact finders', looked at some Shakespeare plays, learnt poems, wrote life stories, painted figures and made large collages of Elizabethan figures, constructed pirates, maps, props for the play, time lines, sand timers, compasses, listened to stories and put together an extensive topic folder.
> (Woods and Jeffrey, 1996 p.126)

Research site visits were determined as and when the researcher felt it appropriate, some being short intense bursts and others being more sporadic. The frequency of time in the field is flexible and intermittent.

In the intensification project, the researcher Geoff, had to be patient to gain access to relevant sites within the school.

> Researching the school for eighteen months allowed the sampling of different temporal phases, that is, the school day, week and year. It was important to spend this length of time in the setting in order to attempt to penetrate the various 'layers of reality' in the school ... I would visit the school for one, two, sometimes three days each week. Different times of day, and days of the week, were chosen for these visits. This approach gave a representative range with which to sample the routine events of school life. At other times, interesting, special, and even extraordinary events were attended. Examples included a special after school meeting of the senior management team, an after school drama production, a paper making exhibition by a visiting artist, an evening meeting for parents and governors, the visit of a government inspector and staff training days.
> (Troman, 1997 p. 46)

Geoff's fieldwork lasted eighteen months in total but he was selective about the sites and contexts to which he needed access. Although he did visit the occasional classroom, once covering for an absent teacher he felt it wasn't appropriate to request observation of lessons or interviews with students. People may well be initially suspicious of a 'total gaze' (Foucault, 1977) and accept more readily only some of their life and work being open to scrutiny (Goffman, 1961). However, the extensive time at this research site increased his familiarity with the staff:

> One context I had not envisaged visiting at the outset of the research was the school sailing club which met one evening each week. Here I could develop relationships with some of the teachers and learn something of their perspectives in a context distant from the school. I attended the club at the invitation of a female teacher who became a key informant.

Central to the intermittent mode is the flexibility to follow 'compelling interests' (Wolcott in Woods, 1986). Bob worked particularly closely with one teacher in the creativity research:

> Judy and I engaged in conversations ranging across politics, biographies, learning strategies, academic work (She was in the middle of her M.A.) and school issues. We met mainly in cafes and chatted for hours. Judy was given copies of any papers that were produced and asked to comment ... In this way we developed a third eye which began to give us insight into our own actions; a form of standing outside oneself ...
> (Jeffrey, 1997 p. 60)

As we talked together she asked questions, offered analysis, made assertions and invoked controversial perspectives. They constructed ideas and understandings together (Jeffrey, 1995):

> In many instances the teacher had not thought about some of the perspectives I contributed and the ensuing conversations became developments of new ways of viewing her practice. In this approach we slid easily between her conscious intentions and new constructions of how her practice could be perceived. Moreover, we re-defined some of her practice in terms that were our own. Apart from claiming some

ownership of the practice we were also able to elaborate the nature of the creative practice in terms of our values. (Jeffrey, 1997 p.66)

Developing an intermittent mode to a research site means gaining the compliance of the inhabitants to enter the site at any time, the gradual opening up of areas for access, the gaining of respondent's trust and commitment to the research, the opportunity to decide during the process of research where to focus and the chance to respond to serendipitous events (Woods, 1996).

The main features of this mode is the flexibility to follow a particular empirical or analytical path, to be able to focus more and more closely on any relevant aspect of a site just as a cinematographer gradually zooms closer and closer on to their preferred subject. The main interest of the researcher, in this mode, is being open to the events of the research process and to be able to pursue particular interests with gusto and to discard those avenues that seem less relevant or interesting. This mode of research combines specific contexts, respondents' interpretations and researcher-respondent discussion and conversation.

A *recurrent* time mode

A recurrent research mode is one where temporal phases formalise the research methodology. These research projects may aim to gain a picture by sampling the same temporal phases, e.g.: beginnings and ends of terms, school celebratory periods such as Christmas, exam periods, inspections. Alternatively, researchers sample on a regular pre-determined basis irrespective of specific events. This is not a snapshot or a zooming approach but more of a documentary approach. There is less flexibility in the frequency of field visits, less progressive focusing for the main objective is to monitor comparison and change. Like the compressed mode every relevant observational detail is recorded but unlike the compressed mode the researcher is able to use the data as a comparison with previous research visits.

One of the frequent purposes of the regular visits is to hold conversations with people to ascertain the similarities and differences over time of processes or specific events. Recurring conversations have a past, present and future, 'How has your perspective changed since we last spoke'?'How have you altered your practice or behaviour since we last spoke'?'What coping strategies have you used'? What do you anticipate being the major issues over the next few months'? The recurrent mode is an opportunity to study a whole cycle such as a school year or a term and assess the balance between the different phases.

Secondly, the recurrent mode is an opportunity to follow the narrative of an experience such as the development of teachers' and learners' artistic skills or a change in gender inequalities over a specific time period and to chart the development, tensions and dilemmas of people in the narrative. A third possibility is to research the effects of change on an institution, group or set of individuals. In this case the researcher might be interested in the effects over time of the introduction of new programmes, policies or routines, implementation effectiveness, inculcation experiences or the effects of specific events. The recurrent mode with its built in time factor assists the unpacking of the relationship between the macro, meso and micro of social structures, for example, during times of reform. One teacher from the inspection research summed up an internal contradiction that threw light upon the effects the inspections were having upon her professional identity;

> I still am worried. I haven't found me yet. I haven't found myself because I do in fact care. I don't feel that I'm working *with* the children any more, I'm working *at* the children but it's not a very pleasant experience. You feel responsible for every part of the school, whether you had anything to do with it or not but at the same time I feel alienated from it all, divorced from it all. Does that make sense? No it doesn't really.
>
> (Alison Year 6 teacher)

Although observation of respondents *in situ* is considered necessary to counteract respondent rhetoric (Atkinson 1990) it is not always possible for researchers to be allowed the extensive time at a site to monitor change. This dilemma is partly resolved by conversations over time, in which researchers reflect back to respondents their previous perspectives and together they explore contradictory behaviours (Jeffrey, forthcoming), where people exhibit over time what appear to be inconsistent reactions and behaviours.

Our research into the effects of Ofsted inspections on primary teachers fitted the recurrent mode as, to some extent, did the stress research. The inspection research began in each school approximately a term before their actual inspection with regular monthly visits for two to three days to complete the collection of perspectives from the identified sample. As the inspection drew closer the frequency increased until the inspection week itself where the researcher stayed in the school all week (see compressed research section above). The sample, head teacher, teachers, support workers and students were all interviewed the week after the inspection and then the frequency was reduced with visits returning to once a month for a term. The main objective of the research was to ascertain the effects of the inspection on the school and the teachers over a lengthy period.

The systematised interviewing of the staff, which focused on their values, current conflicts and the effects of the inspection leading up to it, the actual event and the post inspection period enabled profiles to be developed that showed personal and pedagogic change:

> My attitude to teaching has completely changed since Ofsted. There is no reason for me to be here now except to collect a pay cheque. When I came into teaching that wasn't the reason, it wasn't the reason I was meant to do it. All those things have gone. There is no feeling that this is my vocation, my way of life, that I was meant to do this. I've accepted my lot. I've accepted that this is the way I have to do it. While I was still fighting it was so awful for I was so stressed by it. Now I accept that's the way I have to do it. Although it's depressing, you don't feel so stressed by it. You just get on and do it.   (Brenda Year 2 teacher)

The stress research also collected narratives over time and was able to identify a range of teacher adaptations, for instance, *retreatism, downshifting* and *self actualising* (Troman and Woods 2001).

Systematised recurrent ethnography, particularly when used in a context where people are experiencing unusual and disturbing events, ensures that the respondent and the researcher focus on the passage of time and how this affects the former. In the stress research Geoff found examples of teachers using strategies such as, *personal resourcing, distancing, self-determination, regaining perspective and balance* and *reading and writing* to alleviate the effects of stress (Troman and Woods 2001).

The collection of a wide range of perspectives and experiences is used in ethnographic analysis to assist in an analysis of the complexity of situational life. Although, we have used typologies, for illustrative analysis (Woods et. al. 1997) in full knowledge of the limitations of these approaches (Stronach et. al. 2002) we prioritise contradictory analyses. The analysis of the Ofsted inspection research showed how teachers used opposing coping strategies at the same time:

> We found teacher responses here to be complex, and in some respects contradictory. At the same time as they were experiencing colonisation

and deprofessionalisation the teachers were developing coping strategies. The latter, in themselves, contained apparently contrary behaviours. On the one hand, teachers *distanced* themselves from the Ofsted process in order to maintain their selves and professional identity. At the same time, they *engaged* extensively with the process in order to satisfy the corporate pressures and their faith and commitment to work. These behaviours were generally exhibited simultaneously by the majority of the teachers although within these categories teachers positioned themselves differently.   (Jeffrey and Woods, 1998 p.141)

This analysis arose out of recurrent mode that showed up different and contradictory behaviours. A recurrent mode enables the researcher to compare the different phases of a cycle, to identify change and to develop authentic narratives through respondent reflection and researcher challenge, the researcher taking the role of a narrative film maker.

Conclusion

There are two methodological issues that arise from the differentiation of ethnographic time modalities. The first is how to compensate for the lack of extensive time in the field in the compacted mode and how to resist the familiarity built up over time in the intermittent and recurrent modes. Those engaged in compacted research need to clearly explicate the part played by their subjective engagement for they may well not have lengthy periods of time to collect suitable triangulated data to counter criticisms of researcher bias. However, they can also use other relevant research studies as a broader context through which they can analyse, interpret and theorise.

Conversely, the selective intermittent mode is one in which the researcher is most susceptible to 'going native' (Woods 1986). Respondent validation, team critiques, and memo writing (Jeffrey, 1999) are ways of resolving this issue. The recurrent approach is least troubled by accusations of being too involved but researchers have to ensure that they collect extensive data from some 'key informants' (Woods, 1986) to counter criticisms that they only ever observe surface levels of interaction and respondent perspectives.

A second issue is the fear that this breakdown of 'time' in ethnography could result in the reduction of ethnography to qualitative research. We see ethnographic principles as:

1.   research taking place over time to allow a fuller range of empirical situations

to be observed and analysed and to allow for the emergence of contradictory behaviours and perspectives. Time in the field, alongside time for analysis and interpretation, allows continuous reflections concerning the complexity of human contexts.

2. considering relations between the appropriate cultural, political and social levels of the research site and the individual's and group's/community's agency at the research site.

3. including theoretical perspectives in order to:
   + 'sensitise' field research and analysis;
   + provide an opportunity to use empirical ethnographic research for the interrogation of macro and middle range theories;
   + develop new theory.

The compressed approach would not meet the first criterion. However, researchers would make extensive use of other ethnographies or qualitative studies to allow comparison and interrogation of any analysis.

A research project adopting the selective intermittent approach with its progressive focusing would need to ensure that the second criterion of analysing the influence of multiple discourses is not marginalised. There is a temptation to become so involved with the minutiae of interactions and relations that other influencing factors such as the relevant political, institutional and cultural discourses and structures are ignored. It is therefore important to invoke a range of relevant theories to sensitise the data.

The recurrent research mode, with its emphasis on systemised field visits and on going narrative, may over emphasise distance as researchers focus on recording change and its effects or following the narrative. A consequence of this is that researchers may fail to examine differing reactions to change within individuals and fail to seek out the complex and sometimes contradictory action of people and groups. Theoretical sampling (Strauss and Corbin 1990), where theories developed during the course of analysis are tested at research site, enforces progressive focusing. (Jeffrey, 1999).

The amount of time spent on research is now a central factor of a cost effectiveness discourse in which funders of research want quicker results. They are also less impressed with arguments that the time taken for ethnography or the use of ethnographic methods should be determined by the researcher as the expert in the field. 'Provider capture', in which the professional determines the content and purpose of any research, has been challenged and a 'performativity model' (Ball 2000, Jeffrey 2002) has been introduced, into policy research in particular.

Our response to these demands is to show that there are different types of time in ethnographic research while developing strategies to ensure that ethnographic principles are maintained. For example, a compressed research mode will not, of itself, be enough to find out how effectively a new policy is being implemented but it might provide a snapshot to act as a pilot for further research or be productive enough to confirm or question contemporary research.

A research project, where progressive focusing is essential to tease out complexities and undercurrents would not provide speedy results but interim reports could become more of a feature of the ethnographic process, so satisfying the demand for early analysis. Ethnography is well placed to respond to these demands as the process of ethnography itself is one of data collection, analysis and theorising being carried out simultaneously while continually refining the analysis.

Funders may see research proposals using a recurrent mode in which the field work timetable is fairly fixed in advance, as an expensive option. However, researchers using this mode could indicate clearly the total time needed for a specific research project over a period of time, for example, six months research work over eighteen months. Funding would be limited to actual research time. Our current research designs allocate time to preparation (10%), fieldwork, and evaluation, analysis, (48%) writing reports and papers, (26%) network development and dissemination (8%) and conference attendance and meetings (8%) (CLASP 2002). Researchers would indicate clearly their commitment to other projects over the same period. This strategy may well mean researchers working on more than one project at the same time but, as we identified in the introduction, an anthropological approach to research in education is not feasible today.

Alternatively, we suggest that there could be simultaneous programmes of research, each funded separately and using different but complimentary time frames but situated at the same research sites. We have to show how our methodological approach is flexible and beneficial to funders. Common research sites, such as a particular community, local administrative council or institution, might be propositioned to become long-term research site in which different projects and research teams operated. This would result in some sharing of data and in return the site would have access to a range of continuing analysis to review its operation or culture.

A fitness for purpose needs to be adopted in writing and operating research proposals, whilst at the same time paying attention to ethnographic principles.

Chapter 3

Researching primary teachers' work: Examining policy and practice through interactionist ethnography

Geoff Troman

Introduction

Pollard (1992) when defining the research agenda following the 1988 Education Reform Act (ERA) predicted that the 'core sociological issue of the relationship of the individual to society, of agency and constraint, control and order—will achieve an enhanced place at the centre of studies in primary education' (p.119). And he saw interactionist ethnography as central to that. However, this approach has come under criticism for its failure to achieve this task by linking macro and micro levels of analysis.

When applied to educational research, owing to its orientations on subjectivity, agency, the social construction of reality and the everyday life of participants, symbolic interactionism has been accused of 'empiricism' (Hammersley, 1980)—(eschewing macro-theory) and 'macro-blindness'—(the neglect of constraints on social life which have their origins in social structure) (Whitty, 1974; Sharp, 1982; Troyna, 1994; Power, 1996). However, as Woods (1996, p.48) argues, while the symbolic interactionist focus is on 'the everyday, neglecting social structure and the constraints it places upon actors, is not an essential feature of the approach'. Characteristically, Woods recognises interactionism's potential to 'approach society and social structure from below'(ibid. p. 49). In this approach,

> by monitoring the attribution of meanings as well as how these sustain situations and processes, and how people define and redefine each other's and their own perspectives, patterns may be identified that exhibit personal creativity and external constraint.   (ibid. p49)

My own work (Troman, 1997) has followed this approach, attempting to chart the impact of education policy on teachers in a primary school, enabling a link to be established between policy generated at the macro (societal) level which was experienced at the meso (organisational) and micro (personal) levels.

In such a way, connections were sought between structural and situational factors. These have not been easy to make in the past. Now, owing to legislated initiatives to bring education more in line with economic imperatives, the lines of control, from centre to periphery, are much more visible. In forming links between macro, meso and micro, the ERA has provided an opportunity to study the 'interconnections between political frameworks and school and classroom structure and processes' (Woods, 1996, p.75). Studying these interconnections helps to cultivate the 'sociological imagination'(Mills, 1959).

Arguably, what is needed are detailed studies, informed by symbolic interactionist theory, of what happens when policy reforms are introduced 'into the realm of individual institutions' (Gillborn, 1994, p. 147) in order to discover 'what is going on' (Mac an Ghaill, 1996a). Furthermore, we need to understand the implications the reforms have for teachers and how they are experienced at the meso (organisational) and micro (personal) levels (Reay, 1996). Policy can be more completely understood by looking at its micro aspects to find out more about practitioners and to look at policy with an 'inside-out perspective' (Ball, 1987). Ozga (1990) sees policy analysis as bringing together macro and micro levels of analysis to ensure that the integration of policy analysis with analysis of actors' perspectives provides a 'bigger picture'.

There is a growing tendency in policy theory and research to move from a straightforward conception of policy towards more complex models (Vanegas, 1996). Traditionally, policy was seen as a facticity which was handed down by the powerful and implemented, unproblematically, by the less powerful. Ball characterises this simplistic linear (Tritter, 1995) model as follows:

> Policies as texts 'conjure up' pristine and magical thought worlds of practice—ideal settings in which the intentions of policy makers enter smoothly and unhindered into the minds and actions of the practitioners.   (Ball, 1996a, p.9)

In this view of policy little attempt is made to understand the social processes involved or the perspectives and experiences of those who implement the policy (Vanegas, 1996). Recently new and more complex ways of conceptualising policy have arisen. For instance, there have been calls to focus policy research on the sites of implementation (Bowe et al. 1992; Halpin and Troyna, 1994; Fitz et al. 1994; Raab, 1994). Vanegas (1996) cites Elmore (1996) who argues that policy can be more completely understood by looking at micro aspects of policy to find out more about practitioners. Bowe et al. (1992) who are very critical of top-down models have argued that 'policy formation does not end with the legislative moment, but that it includes the implementation' (Vanegas, 1996, p.3). Ball in developing a definition of policy sociology argues that policy is an economy of power, a set of technologies and practices which are realised and struggled over in local settings. Policy is both text and action, words and deeds, it is what is enacted as well as what is intended. Policies are always incomplete insofar as they relate to or map on to the 'wild profusion' of local practice. Policies are inevitably crude and simple. Practice is sophisticated, contingent, complex and unstable. Policy as practice is 'created' on a trialectic of dominance, resistance and chaos/freedom; that is requirements, prohibitions or incentives, responses and interpretations, and a great deal of 'other' action which is not directly related to policy at all (Ball, 1996a, p.3).

Policy sociology considers policy as a cyclical process and aims to provide an analysis of it in the various phases of the cycle. It offers, too, a means of bridging the macro-micro gap (A. Hargreaves, 1985) since a study focussed on the impact of a range of policies in the 'zone of implementation' (Bowe et al. 1992) will tend to expose the constraints and 'influences of wider societal factors on what teachers do' (Woods, 1996, p.48). Given the lack of studies of primary schools as organisations it seemed timely and appropriate to utilise a policy sociology approach in order to view the impact of a range of recent policies.

My research approach was underpinned by the 'loose body' (Woods, 1996) of symbolic interactionist theory. Symbolic interactionism is seen by some as the polar opposite of functionalist and conflict theories (Worsley, 1970) in that it rejects determinism and views social order as the outcome of the interaction among members of society. While Mead (1934) certainly stresses the importance of socialisation as a shaping force to produce internalised norms of conduct, the individual 'may always act impulsively and creatively in ways that have not been learned from society' (Worsley, 1970, p. 545). Emphasis is on the construction and maintenance of the self (Woods, 1996). The socialised individual is capable of thought, invention and self-determination (Strauss, 1959). Symbolic interactionists therefore concern themselves with the subjective meanings and experiences of individuals (Hitchcock and Hughes, 1989). Blumer (1976) argued that social researchers guided by the theoretical framework of symbolic interactionism would necessarily need to focus on actors' meanings, motivations and interpretations. Like Blumer, Woods stresses the importance of the 'empirical social world', that is, the minute by minute, day to day social life of individuals as they interact together, as they develop understandings and meanings, as they engage in joint action and respond to each other, as they adapt to situations, and as they encounter and move to resolve problems that arise through their circumstances.   (Woods, 1996, p.37)

However, detailed ethnographic studies of schooling often pointed to the inadequacy of macro-perspectives as explanations of the social processes of schooling. Marxist correspondence theory of schooling, for example, was undermined by studies showing that, far from schools producing a docile workforce for capitalism, they actually were a site for resistance and rebellion (Willis, 1977; see Woods, 1996).

However, teacher responses cannot be merely read off from the restructuring policies themselves (Ball, 1994). Teachers in the past have proved to be extremely resistant to imposed change. They have, for instance, deflected and subverted policies rather than implementing them unproblematically (Simons, 1988) On the evidence of other empirical studies of the impact of innovation on teachers, patterns of implementation can be expected to be varied and complex (Bowe et al., 1992; Pollard et al., 1994; Grace, 1995). The changes have to be mediated through the teachers' professional ideologies (Broadfoot and Osborn, 1988) and in the context of their existing work cultures (Mac an Ghaill, 1992). Although the changes are, in the main, legislated, teachers may still have room for 'negotiating' them at school level. How these negotiations are played out is a focus of this chapter.

In the chapter I focus on a case study of one subject manager, derived from the larger primary school ethnography (Troman, 1997). I provide a description and analysis of the perspective of the subject manager in order to show the approach adopted in my study and stress the capacity of interactionist ethnography to illuminate the policy process at the implementation stage. I am, therefore, attempting to realise one of the 'promises' of symbolic interactionism detailed by Woods, 1996).

Methods

This case study is based on data collected during eighteen months of fieldwork, in a primary school. The school, Meadowfields, is located on the outskirts of an English South Midlands market town and had 450 pupils with a staff of seventeen teachers. Access to the school to carry out the research was granted by the Headteacher and senior management team following negotiations with them. While usually being in the role of researcher I sometimes had to adopt other roles in the school. For example, I occasionally stood in for teachers in some classes or worked with small groups of children on specific projects. The data were derived from informal conversations, interviews, observations and school documents (curriculum policy statements, governors' meeting minutes, school development plan). Data collection took place in a variety contexts including, staffroom, staff meetings, senior management team meetings, headteacher's office and inservice education and training days for the teachers. Tape recordings of conversations, meetings and interviews were transcribed and analysed and observations were recorded in field notes. Ongoing analysis of verbal data and observational notes informed subsequent data collection and enabled 'progressive focusing' (Glaser and Strauss, 1967) and 'spiralling insights' (Lacey, 1976) to develop. Though the case study reported here focuses on a subject manager's responses to the impact of several educational policies, the wider study was concerned with the restructuring of teachers' work and the impact of this on their professional and personal identities and on their occupational cultures. By concentrating on a single case I realise that claims of generalisability, or of proof with respect to theory would be inappropriate (Hammersley et al. 1993; Gomm et al. 1998). I seek merely to explore macro—micro links and illuminate the policy implementation process using empirical data from one case. The power of the single case should not be underestimated (Wolcott, 1995).

The subject manager's work

Bowe et al. (1992) argue that the intensification of work in the secondary school has produced conflict through the separation of managers and teachers. In this situation, it is those teachers who are senior managers, but also members of the teaching staff (for example, deputy headteachers and members of the senior management team) who are caught between management and workers and experience considerable conflict owing to this role. The managerial role provides its own frustrations as occupiers of it 'now stand in a dual relation to the staff and to senior management. (They) 'understand' both parties, stand between and inhabit their two worlds, but feel unable to secure a permanent reconciliation' (ibid. p. 149). This kind of tension is likely to be experienced more acutely in the primary school where, in the new role of subject manager,[1]

---

1   A large proportion of the policy document 'Primary Matters' (Ofsted, 1994) is devoted to rehearsing solutions designed to rectify the failure to implement the National Curriculum more fully. One cause identified was poor curriculum management and what was recommended was more and better management

cont./

the boundaries between management and teachers might be expected to be less clearly demarcated than in secondary schools. Indeed, new managerial roles in the primary school are providing opportunities for teachers and are offering a range of new professional identities, but the adoption of these is proving problematical (Maclure, 1993). Some aspects of the new teacher role provide opportunities for role enhancement, while others threaten to deskill teachers. There is, in the new role of subject manager, a potential for role tension and conflict. Although Woods et al. (1997) argue that the primary teacher's traditional role as generalist class teacher was diffuse and inherently conflictual, there are indications from recent research that, in the subject manager role, these features have been exacerbated (Webb and Vulliamy, 1995). Those teachers who are subject managers, and, as I have argued previously (Troman, 1996), form the majority of the profession, were likely to experience heightened conflicts and role tensions for the following reasons:

+   The introduction of market principles and management-led reform into primary schools is potentially at odds with the existing dominant ideologies of teaching (Ball, 1994);

+   The unceasing drive to raise educational standards has ensured greatly raised expectations of the subject manager role (Webb and Vulliamy, 1995);

+   Official role expectations for the subject manager are now clearly specified. More explicit job descriptions now embody policy maker and headteacher definitions of the teacher's role (Troman, 1996);

+   Accountability procedures, such as school inspections, now focus in a major way on the subject manager role (Webb and Vulliamy, 1996).

+   The changes in teachers' work has involved 'galloping role inflation' (Campbell and Neill, 1994). Apart from their considerable managerial role, the subject managers are also class teachers having to implement the National Curriculum, assessment and testing;

+   With the growth of school development planning, the work of subject managers is linked more clearly with specific development targets (Webb and Vulliamy, 1996);

+   With the demise of advisory teachers (Webb and Vulliamy, 1996), and

of teachers' work. The key to this was seen to be, as in previous reports, to promote the importance of the management aspects of the role of the curriculum co-ordinators. These were renamed as 'subject managers' because 'co-ordinators (was) too limited a description' (ibid. p.9, para. 37), as it certainly was if all of the likely elements of the co-ordinator's role which emerged in the 1992 discussion paper (DES, 1992) were included in it.

the decline of LEA provided INSET, many subject managers may be solely responsible for the school-based development of their subject;

◆ Changes in organisation and role are taking place in a context marked by contradictions. For, whilst top-down managerialism is evident and the power and authority of the primary headteacher is undiminished, it co-exists alongside the discourses and practices of devolved management, flattened hierarchies, participative decision-making, collaborative work cultures, shared professional learning and teacher empowerment (Grace, 1995);

◆ The traditional factors of low levels of time, authority and resources on the co-ordinator's role seem likely to remain (Kinder and Harland, 1991);

◆ Role expectations are now being transformed into role obligations and role tensions are becoming constraints (Woods et al. 1997).

In the following section I explore the perceptions of Elizabeth, the Maths co-ordinator at Meadowfields. Her perspective, revealed through conversations, illuminates the changing nature of her work as a subject manager and her interpretation of the official version of the subject manager role. It exposes the ambiguities of intensification and the conflicts and tensions in the new role. Before I undertake this analysis, I will provide some contextualisation.

Background

All the teachers at the school, with the exception of newly qualified teachers, had a curriculum responsibility which included the supervision and monitoring of the work of their colleagues. However, it was Elizabeth who, in my estimation, approximated most closely to the official model of the 'good teacher' (Troman, 1996). Elizabeth is fifty years old and has been in teaching for approximately thirty years. She spent a short time in secondary schools before moving to the primary sector where she has worked for the major part of her career. As a subject manager she had not received any management training. At Meadowfields a general pattern seemed to be for the teachers to acquire additional management responsibilities as their careers progressed in the school. A key time in the allocation of these responsibilities had been in the aftermath of an inspection by HMI who instructed the school to formulate a new school development plan which 'should include the redefinition of staff roles and responsibilities'. Co-ordinators of subjects which had been most criticised by HMI were replaced. Elizabeth had been appointed by the Headteacher following ERA as a change agent to facilitate his restructuring of the school and in this role he described her as the 'first chisel in the rock'. She was a member of the senior management team and, like her colleagues, was a full-time class teacher. She and other subject managers were, of course, heavily involved in implementing all of the measures of the ERA, measures which in terms of policy had been the subject of constant changes since 1988. As subject manager for mathematics she was responsible for developing the subject throughout the school, and this involved leading a large programme of school-based INSET. Additionally, she was responsible for the teacher appraisal scheme and the ordering, purchase and allocation of resources for all subjects. She was highly thought of by all of the other teachers I had conversations with. When asked to recall concrete incidents when a subject co-ordinator had helped them with professional development, they frequently mentioned her name. While her teaching commitment, managerial responsibilities and her membership of the senior management team led me to identify her as a subject manager, her perspective on herself, her work and the social relations of the school, as shown through analysis of conversations, showed ambivalence towards the new role. She might be considered, therefore, as a partial, or even reluctant, teacher/manager, for whilst being seen as successful in the new managerial role, she felt uncomfortable with many aspects of her new expanded and intensified work. She would also reflect critically on the impact of managerialism on her and the school. There was, therefore, evidence of role conflict in her perspective. She was not completely 'caught' (Ball, 1994) by the new managerialism and still felt drawn to her former role as a creative and relatively autonomous generalist class teacher (Woods, 1995). Her feelings about the subject manager role were, therefore, suggestive of an 'ambivalent enhancement'. Her positive feelings related to greater expertise and ownership and control. These appeared to meet her personal needs. Negative feelings were associated with the intensification of work and reduced ownership and control. I shall examine each of these in turn.

Positive feelings

Greater expertise

Elizabeth appeared to enjoy her role when helping other teachers by giving advice informally. She had produced a voluminous resource pack for each teacher to draw on in their teaching. In the INSET sessions she led she demonstrated her expertise by enthusiastically communicating her views about and methods of teaching mathematics through investigations. She felt this method of teaching, although requiring more skill, should be adopted throughout the school.

However, many of the teachers resisted this approach and continued using published Maths schemes. Elizabeth's involvement in planning was not restricted to topic and lesson planning. As a member of the senior management team, she was closely involved with school development planning and the formulation of school policy. Indeed one of her first managerial tasks at the school, following ERA, was to formulate a Maths policy. In previous posts, she 'really hadn't been aware of school policy', and certainly hadn't written one, but at this school she showed a measure of pride in having done it:

> I think the first thing I did when I came here was write the school's Maths policy. There were no guidelines, real sort of clear guidelines. So I went on an Open University Maths diploma course which was a great help. I worked with a couple of other people to get some ideas together but its one of those things it was best working on your own though it was supposed to be involving everybody and everyone's ideas to make the whole thing work. It really wasn't feasible because there was no time to do it in school. It had to be done at home. So, it's pretty much my document and now, of course, that's totally out of date.

While feeling proud of using new knowledge and skills in Maths teaching in order to write policy, Elizabeth seemed to recognise here that the new managerialism should be accomplished collaboratively, rather than individually. Elizabeth was almost apologetic in her admission that this managerial task was accomplished alone, even though intensification of work had forced the situation and she recognised that, in some tasks, solitary working may be superior to collegial effort (A. Hargreaves, 1994).

Ownership and control

Elizabeth obviously enjoyed some parts of her work as a manager and seemed to possess some 'natural' management skills:

> It's nice to have a say in what goes on in school, and I think I've been here long enough to know how things happen, how people tick and what's accepted and what's not, and how to get around people, or talk to people or whatever. I just like to be in the know as well.

She recognised that management roles, while providing opportunities for being in control, can contribute to further intensification of work:

> ... enjoyable, I suppose you could use that word. If I wasn't doing it, like if I wasn't doing Maths in that co-ordinator's role, I'd be very irritated by perhaps what another co-ordinator would do, and that sort of feeling. I'd feel that I wanted to be in charge of it even though, sometimes the workload is heavy. But, I think sometimes I could do without bits of the management role.

As a teacher governor, she was unsure about potential managerial domination by the lay governors, but did see that there could be benefits:

> Governors have got better management skills than we have. They're more aware of budgeting than we are. Perhaps we can palm off some of these jobs onto them and let us control what happens in school and the education side of it.

Elizabeth felt that there was a collaborative culture in the school, and that she gained from it. She not only gave advice but also received it:

> I think the collaboration here is very good. I feel I can go and talk to most people in a very casual way and get ideas. They're very forthcoming.

Negative feelings

Intensification of work

She clearly recognised the recent intensification of her work and gave many indications of pressure, tension and stress, in phrases such as:

> heavy workload ... being asked to do too much ... extra jobs ... no finish/no end to it ... pressure on you ... all the time spent trying to do your best ... now its two topics a term and its a nightmare ... God I haven't done this and I haven't done that and I've got to do that ... being asked to do too much ... getting in the way of my private life ... feeling dizzy/shell-shocked at the end of the day ... we seem to spend most of our time going round

in circles ... I didn't do half as much work out of school as I do now ... making me rush things ... its taking longer and longer at home to do the stuff, like I say its lucky that my husband is a teacher ... .children aren't being taught what's in the plans in some cases because there isn't time to do it ... I don't think I'm teaching as well as I used to simply because I'm being asked to do too much ... it doesn't make for a very smooth, calm person ... you're fighting against it all the time ... pressure on you to get things up and running.

Although experiencing intensification of work arising from largely managerial tasks, she still put the children in her class first:

It's (managerial work) getting in the way of my private life. I think I end up feeling dizzy at the end of the day because so many other things have happened, like some stock will arrive, or somebody'll want to see somebody about something or the Head will want to see you about something, or you're meeting with somebody else, and at the end of the day I feel quite sort of shell-shocked sometimes. But it really doesn't get in the way of what's happening in the class because that's got to come first or else the school falls apart, because you can't cope in the classroom then. I think everybody has days when they're going sort of off the cuff and that can happen any time. You can have a late night, friends call round, but the majority of my time outside school, the extra time, it's taken up, I don't call the extra time for the kids, that's always going to be there, more times taken up with sort of management co-ordinating stuff.

In his study of a primary school, Hayes (1994) found some teachers who were reluctant to engage in collaborative whole-school decision-making, and assume further managerial responsibilities. This was for the very practical reason that participation would demand extra time commitments which, the teachers believed, would result in their having reduced time for planning and teaching their classes. The teachers were class-focused rather than whole-school focused. And, therefore, were 'restricted' rather than 'extended professionals' (Hoyle, 1974). While this was true of some of the teachers at Meadowfields, Elizabeth seems to have partly resolved the tension between managerial and teacher roles by displacing some of the extra management tasks into her personal life thereby further increasing intensification. She blamed herself for not 'being as quick as others' to complete tasks and often took work home. She felt fortunate that her teacher husband understood the pressures and did not complain. Some of her female colleagues completed their work at school by staying behind for several hours so that they could avoid feelings of guilt induced by complaints, from non-teaching partners, about bringing work home.

Elizabeth felt under pressure to fill in many planning sheets:

> It's just an extra job. Because Art is part of our topic work, we have to list Light (a Science subject) as part of our topic. So we record it on our Art sheet, Science sheet and Humanities sheet. Now, Art's connected to music, so you're writing things out four or five times.

However, as part of management, she participated in making the decision to have multiple planning sheets. Indeed she required the teachers to submit their Maths planning to her and thereby contributed to the intensification of their work:

> I'm putting pressure on people. I'm just thinking well they're not actually doing much extra work they're just putting it all on one side of paper and it's building up a scheme of work. But it's asking somebody to do something else.

She notes, too, the artificiality of the system which separates managerial planning from teaching:

> You're duplicating planning, and sometimes it has little to do with what you're doing in the classroom, and sometimes it's not needed for what you're doing in the classroom.

Reduced ownership and control

Elizabeth previously worked in a private international school in France which was organised on democratic principles. She now believed that owing to the veneer of democracy and the extent of micro-political activity, Meadowfields had fallen short of genuine and equal participation:

Before I came here I was at an *avant-garde* school. It was brilliant. They didn't have a head they had a chairperson, who was voted in for two years. Anybody could have been chairperson and everybody had a say in how the school was run. It took a long time to get anything done but at least you felt you were working for the school not an authority—it was independent. It was a small school. It wouldn't work on a big scale. There was only about 180 kids. No decisions were made at a meeting until you had time to go away and think about it. You weren't bamboozled into saying 'yes' or 'no' straight way. You could come back to the next meeting and vote on it.

If Elizabeth was losing some control in decision-making, this was also occurring in school policy formulation:

The county is saying that two sides of A4 is all you need for your policy documents, but it can't be very clear if it's just two sides. What I wrote wasn't just my ideas it included a lot of some very clever people's thinking in Maths and how it should be taught. I thought that was very valuable— but two sides, that's meaningless. But that's what we're supposed to be doing so that's what we are doing.

Elizabeth's teaching philosophy seems at odds with 'technicist' versions, yet she recognises that in her teaching now she must on occasions depart from her child-centred approach in order to engage in managerial tasks, such as planning and recording and reaching targets, which have been specified by others. She recognises that she has lost some ownership of pedagogy, and that bureaucracy had eclipsed teaching and eroded personal relationships:

You could do a topic for a whole term and all the kids do lots of investigative work, and lots of testing out their theories, lots of making stuff to see if it works and really delving quite deeply into a subject, but not just the facts of a subject but to understand how things worked. And that was fine spending a term on a topic. Now it's two a term and it's a nightmare. We've got to do sound and light in seven weeks. You can't do a lot of getting to know what sound is all about and then do any really valuable investigations in that time. You've got to be feeding them information, in a way, to a certain extent you've got to give information.

Some kids know because they catch on more quickly and they're making connections, but those little mites at the bottom—you're just shoving stuff at them I feel sometimes. The main focus was the children and now it seems to have shifted from that a lot on to how you record what you're teaching and how you record what the children are doing and how you plan so far ahead for everything, that you almost forget the kids that are involved in it.

In writing a recent school policy, to accommodate the recent national policy changes, she felt deskilled and frustrated. She expected external 'experts' to eventually reveal the 'perfect' policy:

> We've had no training for this, that's why it's so frustrating not knowing you're doing the right thing. I've spent years and years trying to do it (formulate policy)...there's nothing clear from the Maths team (LEA Maths advisors and advisory teachers) ... they just give out ideas and you have to work it out yourselves. That's a bit more work. If we're going to have to do it like that why don't they just give us the sheet and say, 'There you are.'

Here the dependency on external 'experts' potentially undermined professional judgement and reduced control. Elizabeth is also losing control of how she carries out her work as subject manager. Since the inspection, she was expected to undertake classroom observation of colleagues for monitoring and appraisal. HMI had included this strong expectation in their report and the Headteacher had been instructed to include it in the job descriptions of senior management and to give co-ordinators the authority to carry it out. A 'floating' Deputy Headteacher form of organisation made a small amount of non-contact time available for this task:

> What's meant to happen now is that I'm able to go into different areas to work with people—it's a much more organised set up. It's actually working in classrooms with people. I worked with their planning but I haven't worked in classrooms with anybody yet and that's part of the brief since the inspection. I don't know how that's going to work—it's going to be a bit delicate I think because I don't want to tread on anyone's toes.

The new managerial role here stands in contrast to older versions of professionalism in which classroom autonomy was central. Elizabeth respected the autonomy of colleagues and gave it priority over monitoring and advisory work. Thus, as in Campbell's (1988) study, 'paradoxically, from the point of view of curriculum development, the concept of the class teacher's 'autonomy' in curricular matters was to some extent shared by the (co-ordinators) themselves, despite the fact that the consequence of their curriculum development activities was to bring such a concept into question' (p.227). Elizabeth hesitated to enter into classrooms in her advisory role to work alongside colleagues because this might involve her in making evaluations of her colleagues' teaching:

> It's just the way you approach people isn't it. You work with them rather than showing them this is the way to do it. That's not what you do. You can't go in and say that to a teacher who has been teaching for n number of years and imply that they're not doing it the right way. I must say I haven't solved that problem yet. I haven't actually gone into a classroom yet.

Holding these reservations, yet having to monitor the work of colleagues in her managerial role, she relied on unobtrusive means of evaluation:

> You get their plans and it all seems fine but it's not being done that way, and that came out in the inspectors' report as well, that what is happening in the policy is not happening in the classroom. Not in one but in all classrooms. And then just by—it's almost like being a spy but it's an accidental spy—so you see things on blackboards or see peoples' worksheets and just think, 'Oh my God that's happening'. And how do you stop it happening?

She was also uncertain how to proceed on the strength of evidence from colleagues' planning:

> I think they know they have got some gaps in their planning and I can go and talk to them about it. But I don't want to go and tread on their toes. It's got to be done very carefully and I haven't put my mind to that yet.

Elizabeth's previous experience of being observed herself by a colleague warned her of the potential falseness of classroom observation:

I hate people watching the way I teach. You really feel you're being seen with a critical eye and that's got to be avoided really. I remember Frances came and she asked if she could come in and listen to the language that was used. Not just mine, but I think the language in the class. So I said, 'That's alright'. But when she was there I didn't speak the way I do normally at all. It was all totally false, and I thought, 'well Christ if she thinks that's what it's like all the time?'.

Elizabeth can provide a rationalisation for the gap between policy and practice in the school and can sympathise with her colleagues who cut corners because of the intensification of work, their educational values, or their lack of subject confidence and expertise:

In some cases, children aren't being taught what's on the plans, in some cases because there isn't time to do it, and in other cases because people don't believe that what's on the plans is what the children should be taught. It's over a year now since we had an INSET on this aspect of Maths and this sort of thing shouldn't be happening at all. But people forget, and if it's not your subject and you don't feel too confident you fall back on old methods and the things that you did at school. I do that as well.

There was also recognition that the production of documentation which accompanied bureaucracies and managerialist cultures had ascendancy in this school, over issues central to teaching and learning:

... as long as you've got your planning in place, and its all nicely written up, what you get through to the kids is secondary. Partly because you've hardly got time to think about them, you're thinking so much about the planning.

Conclusion

What then can this analysis of Elizabeth's perspective on her role add to our knowledge of the changing nature of primary teachers' work, and one aspect of the intensification thesis; the professionalisation versus deprofessionalisation debate? Certainly the analysis broadly supports Campbell's (1988) findings on role conflict in the co-ordinator's work. It also confirms Pollard et al. (1994) and Woods et al. (1997) on teachers' feelings towards their new role. What, I feel, the in-depth analysis of a single case adds is an insight into the complexity of the changes which are taking place. Pollard et al. (op cit.) present the teachers in their large sample as being for or against the National Curriculum. When reporting teacher responses to changes in their role, the authors found that a majority of teachers report feeling deprofessionalised because of their experience of managerial aspects of the role. These included administration, increased planning, loss of spontaneity and child responsiveness in their teaching, increased stress and anxiety, a strong sense of imposition of external priorities and a feeling of loss of autonomy and creativity. The authors also show that the most common form of teacher accommodation to the changes, 'incorporation', involved the teachers in implementing the reforms but not sacrificing values and practices that were really important to them. Furthermore, a minority of teachers drew on an 'emergent professionalism' and felt that this had been enhanced by restructuring. These findings present a view of teacher response in which some feel empowered or affirmed while some feel deskilled or deprofessionalised. Their data also suggests that some teachers, the 'incorporators', may feel a range of these. What the case-study of Elizabeth shows is this complexity of response which is the source of the role conflict and resultant stress of which there were indications Elizabeth was experiencing.

How then can this complexity be explained? One approach would be to see Elizabeth as being reprofessionalised as an education manager. Harris, (1995) in a study of women, in the public and private sectors, who had recently been promoted to management, noted contradictions in their accounts of the process of becoming a manager. She explained these as revealing conflicts or tensions in the work roles they occupied, or the complexity of perspective reflected the circumstances of uncertainty or confusion in which the new managers worked. This situation produced a sense of disorientation, bafflement or puzzlement as they attempted to adapt their changing roles (Harrison et al. 1992). She also suggests that her interview material indicates a sense of transition in the subject's personal biography which has to take account of discontinuities while retaining a sense of continuity of self.

Woods (1995) writes of a 'liminal' stage, a kind of betwixt and between in which teachers mourn the loss (Nias, 1991) of some aspects of the old as they struggle to adapt to the new. For Woods, contradictions in teacher accounts can, partly, be considered as an expression of the teachers' experience of 'liminality'. In conditions of rapid cultural change the production of professional subjectivities is a shifting scene (Mac an Ghaill, 1996b). Professionalism must, therefore be considered as a dynamic concept. The production of identity is both a personal and a social process (Berger, 1966; Woods, 1983). Selves are constructed through interaction with others. In primary teaching, professional and personal identity intermingle, each feeding into the other. It might be expected, therefore, that the restructuring of work and of personal relations, that this entails, through the formation of changed organisations and occupational cultures will have implications for teachers' professional identities. In the new workplace the new managerial forms sit, sometimes uncomfortably, on top of old work practices and ideologies (Menter et al. 1997). Although Elizabeth saw opportunities in her new role, and was 'humanistic rather than managerialist in approach', the new work was a source of tensions (Woods et al. 1997, p.91). However, this brand of 'critical humanistic managerialism could be seen as a positive base on which to develop managerial practices in primary schools' (ibid. p. 91).

Research in education policy studies has, for too long, ignored the empirical reality of policy implementation in the primary school (Pollard, 1992). The 'rich underlife of social processes attending the recontextualisation of policy' (Ball, 1994, p.19) has, therefore, been neglected. This chapter has sought to address this neglect. In doing so, my method has been more bottom up in that I have tried, through the experiences and perspective of one teacher, to chart the 'effects' (rather than outcomes) of policy in the school and to understand the actions and motives of the implementors, and 'what takes place' from the inside (Fitz et al. 1994, p.64). I have shown how official policy is interpreted by a teacher, at school level. Policy goals are not directly translated into action, but are transformed when they are recontextualised (Ball, 1994). I have exposed some of the struggles over the implementation of policy. In focusing on how the subject manager dealt with the problems that policies raised for her, I have shown something of the impact that the policies have on her consciousness and sense of self. This teacher's response indicates 'creative social action not robotic reactivity' (Ball, 1994, p.19). This analysis has attempted to link the macro (via the meso) to the micro, showing how agency and structure are implicit in one another. However, the restructuring of definitions of the work of teaching, teachers and their work is being carried out, sometimes at great personal cost to individuals. I do not, therefore, seek to celebrate agency at the expense of structure.

It is possible to use the data and analysis of the Meadowfields case study in order to interrogate the intensification thesis. In empirical research on changes in teachers' work, two arguments are frequently used. There are those who claim that the restructuring of education brings work changes which contribute to enhanced professionalism in teachers. Alternatively, it is argued that the historically inevitable process of intensification of teachers' work is occurring. Arguments stressing professionalisation emphasise greater teacher professionalism.

Woods (1995), while pointing out teachers' positive reactions to the National Curriculum, notes that the research evidence showing massive work overload, which primary teachers in the English education system have encountered since the introduction of the ERA, lends a great deal of support to the intensification thesis. On the basis of the Meadowfields case study, it seems reasonable to claim that intensification was a major feature of the teachers' working lives. However, it has to be asked, were the teachers becoming deskilled and deprofessionalised as a result? While the teachers were subjectively experiencing apparently worsening work conditions, they were also adopting new roles and responsibilities which required not only new levels of professional skill, but also enhanced professional commitment. Others who have produced evidence which (on the face of it) would support the intensification thesis, have argued that the teachers in their studies were not being deprofessionalised. Campbell et al. (1991, p.31), for instance, concluded a study of infant teachers' work by claiming that '... our evidence suggests that the imposed change of the National Curriculum, far from de-skilling and de-professionalising the teachers was, on the contrary, seen by them as extending their skills and increasing their professionalism'. Osborn et al. (1994), although finding a majority of teachers feeling deskilled, did identify a fifth of their large sample of teachers as feeling empowered by the changes. Acker (1990, p.270) was 'loath to discuss their (the teachers) perceptions' of enhanced professionalism 'as false consciousness' and concluded that 'their skill feels real to them and looks real to me'. Woods' (1995a) teachers 'recognised intensification for what it was' but 'retained their reflective ability' and had the self-determination to continue their creative and progressive project (p.65). Hargreaves (1994) finds evidence both to support and refute the intensification argument. His teachers experienced both enhanced professionalism and intensification leading to deskilling. Cooper and MacIntyre (1996), in a study of secondary teachers, show how the teachers extended their professional skills through collaborative working since the introduction of the National Curriculum, which was resulting in shared professional learning and critical reflection on teaching. Evans et al. (1994) noted some teachers in their study, while experiencing the stress of intensified work, becoming 'extended' professionals (Hoyle, 1974) as they improved their whole-school planning, assessment and Science teaching skills. However, the majority of the teachers in Evans et al.'s study were not found to be responding to the challenges, or taking up the opportunities, for 'extended' professionalism, thrown up in their restructured work. The authors concluded that this group of teachers experienced stress because of the tension between their child/classroom centred philosophy and the official expectation that they engage in whole-school work. It is the view of the authors that teachers experiencing this mode of deskilling not only slow down the reform process but also miss opportunities for professional enhancement. Others, however, have interpreted this form of teacher response as evidence of enhanced professionalism.

However, management hegemony and intensification could not be assumed in the school. Though systems and culture were changing, control of teachers' work was the outcome of struggle. This kind of process has been termed the 'dialectics of control' by Giddens (1987, and in Reay, 1996, p.1). New roles were not unproblematically occupied and implemented by the teachers. Teacher compliance was not automatic. Resistances occurred because some of the teachers were unwilling or unable to fulfil their new role expectations. Elizabeth, one of the 'new professionals', while feeling ambivalent about her managerial role, and experiencing conflict and stress, was unwilling to engage with aspects of it which entailed appraisal (even though she was head of appraisal), monitoring, and review of colleagues. She was clinging on to her old notions and culture of individualism, and respected colleagues who wanted to retain some individual discretion, control, and autonomy in their work. Teachers confronted with tensions and unwilling to occupy the new roles could be viewed as deskilled (Evans et al. 1994). However, Woods et al. (1997) see the successful transformation of these as evidence of an extended and enhanced professionalism. Teaching technicians (Apple, 1986), on the other hand, would not be likely to experience the tensions of their restructured work and would implement official policy unproblematically.

The source of teachers', tensions were largely at the societal level:

> Macro phenomena are implicated in every day micro interactions (Giddens, 1987); the point being that staff relationships within schools need to be conceptualised not simply in terms of interaction within school walls but also as the playing out of governmental and local policy and politics.   (Reay, 1996, pp. 1-2; see also Gillborn, 1994)

I have tried to convey the complexity of one teacher's responses to the introduction of policy on newly defined roles at Meadowfields school. I conclude that an unproblematical reading of the changes is not possible. We are not faced with a straightforward bi-polar choice, of professionalisation versus intensification, in order to sum up these responses (Hargreaves, 1994). While some intensification is certainly taking place, it is accompanied by both deskilling and reskilling/upskilling. Elizabeth, therefore, was simultaneously being professionalised and deprofessionalised (Woods et al. 1997). In other words, restructuring has set in train a process of reprofessionalisation. Clearly then, labour process theory and the intensification thesis are inadequate in order to conceptualise the changes taking place to teacher professionalism at Meadowfields (Hargreaves, 1994; Campbell and Neill, 1994; Woods, 1995).

What, then would constitute an adequate explanation? I agree with Hargreaves (1993, p.92). that 'further studies in which other theories and perspectives in addition to those concerned with the nature of the labour process may need to be acknowledged as important for our understanding'. These other theories, on the basis of this case study, are likely to be ones that can more adequately embrace conceptions of both structure and agency. Frameworks having this kind of explanatory capacity are interpretative theories of the self and coping strategies. This is why continued research in the interactionist ethnographic mode should be undertaken in order to further examine theory, policy and practice.

Section II—Policy, representation and dissemination
Chapter 4

How to 'describe' ethnographic research sites

Bob Jeffrey

Introduction

Ethnographic data collection includes 'factual descriptions', impressionist field notes, recorded conversations, imaginative memos, comparisons with other research and the archiving of relevant documents. Analysis is carried out contemporaneously alongside data collection. The latter assists in selecting foci as well as becoming the basis for a representation of findings. Much of this work is problematic in terms of: the researcher as a research instrument, (Ball, 1990a; Denzin, 1998; Wolcott, 1995) validity claims (Hammersley, 1992; Strauss and Corbin, 1990) and the representation of reality (Woods, 1996; Atkinson, 1990). Another specific problem is that given that ethnography is descriptive explanation (Hammersley, 1992) we firstly need to address the problem of *how* we can describe what is happening rather than attempt initially to explain what is happening (Woods, 1986). We suggest that the collection of diverse behaviours, practices and perspectives can assist the process of learning how to describe what is happening. Firstly, however some details of the particular research project through which we will examine these strategies is needed.

The Ofsted inspection research

The research focused on the experiences of teachers in six schools receiving their first inspection from Ofsted (The Office for Standards in Education). This is an independent organisation set up by the British government to carry out standardised inspections of every State school. They began a second round of inspections in 1998 and we returned to two of the schools to continue the research. Each school was visited regularly for at least six months prior to their inspection and six months after the inspection. A total of over eighty teachers had discussions with the researcher although a core group of twenty had as many as six conversations with us. We talked to head teachers, inspectors, teachers, teaching assistants, governors, parents and pupils. A book of the whole research (Jeffrey and Woods, 1988) is available and a summary has also been published (Woods and Jeffrey, 1998). Ethnographic methods were employed, including:

the collection of relevant documents and statistics; participant's perspectives; respondent validation and diaries; and the construction of observational field notes, memos, papers presented at conferences. However the actual classroom and school inspection, which was carried out over one week, was not observed directly. The researcher stayed in the school staff room during the period the inspectors were in the school and consequently no specific inspection practices were observed.

Diverse behaviours, practices and perspectives

Behaviours, practices and perspectives can be discerned within specific contexts and across different contexts. Researchers may observe similar or diverse behaviours practices and perspectives within and between contexts. An example of the former might be Blumer and Hauser's findings that films can be a powerful influence upon children and an example of diverse data behaviours practices and perspectives would be that they found that films may exert influences in diametrically opposed directions (Blumer and Hauser, 1933, p. 201). We focus on diverse behaviours, practices and perspectives, opposing or alternative practices. They are connected to each other by context: e.g.: family, school community; by choice of researcher focus, e.g.: literacy practices, teaching methodology; and research conceptualisation, e.g.: memberships symbols, rituals, cultures. We have identified three analytical foci, opposing, multiple and contradictory actions.

Opposing behaviours, practices and perspectives

Opposing behaviours, practices or perspectives exist between individuals, between groups and between communities are ones in which there is a significant polarisation or distancing of a specific relationship in values, beliefs and practices. The recording and analysis of the nature of these oppositions may reveal superficial or fundamental differences and the representation of them is one of the first challenges in describing what is happening. In our case the opposing forces were clearly delineated. An external, individually unknown group of inspectors examined the school over five days using an unfamiliar framework. The schools were notified six months in advance.

The dominant response from teachers concerning the inspection was one of anxiety concerning the process of the inspection and the consequences for their professional lives and for their futures. The inspection criteria and procedures were new and considered in conflict with many of the 'child centred' pedagogies

(Siraj-Blatchford and Siraj-Blatchford, 1995) used by the teachers and the numerical grading of teacher competence was considered an anathema by most of the teachers.

We firstly made an effort to seek out oppositions and then attempted to account for them. After obtaining the teachers perspectives we interviewed the leader of each of the inspection teams and putting both sets of data together we ascertained differences in values and pedagogic practices between the new Ofsted Framework and the teachers' professional beliefs work. These were categorised under the headings of knowledge, pedagogies, assessment and culture.

A.   *Knowledge.*

Ofsted Values	Teacher Values
Prescribed National Curriculum	Negotiated Curriculum
Controlled National Curriculum	Flexible and Autonomous Practices
Emphasis on Products	Emphasis on Process
Subject-based curriculum	Child-centred, Holistic, Integrative
Systematisation, Standardisation, Uniformity	Differences, Diversity

B.   *Pedagogy*

Ofsted Values	Teacher Values
Transmissional	Creative
Behaviourist	Constructivist Learning Theory
Formal	Informal Contexts
Examination	Support
Instant performance	Learning takes time

C.   *Assessment (of pupils and teachers)*

Ofsted Values	Teacher Values
Formal	Informal
Quantitative	Qualitative
Standardised	Localised
Periodic tests	Continuous
Hierarchical Examination	Collective Engagement, Self-Assessment
Simplicity	Complexity

D   *Culture*

Ofsted Values	Teacher Values
Competition and Individualism,	Collegiality
Detachment	Involvement
Blame	Support
Managerialism	Professionalism
Control	Self-Regulation
Consumer	Producer

(Jeffrey and Woods, 1998 p. 82)

The collection of alternative perspectives from those in direct conflict with the community group—the inspectors—enabled us to explain through description the reasons for the teacher-Ofsted 'stand off'.

We also considered it necessary to seek out diverse perspectives in order to challenge and constrain the researcher's 'bias'. Immersion into this particular community, one experiencing what appeared to these teachers to be an inappropriate use of an outside force, caused the ethnographic researcher to empathise and sympathise with those living through the experience, particularly as I had been a primary school teacher. It is not possible to 'wash away' (Woods, 1986) or suspend one's experiences, values and beliefs. Indeed it is argued that attempting to do so would diminish the quality of the data collected (Ball, 1990a). The collection of diverse perspectives forces the researcher to consider how to represent opposing behaviours and practices. We chose to focus on the differences between the Ofsted inspectors and the primary teachers in terms of values related to knowledge, pedagogy, assessment and culture, which rooted the research findings in empirical examples rather than just presenting a picture of opposing forces. At the same time the researcher's sympathies were not marginalised as in suspending beliefs but restructured in terms of empathy and used as a tool of ethnographic representation as in this example from field notes included in the publication of our book:

Two teachers, both black, were visited after school on dip day by two inspectors. Tracy was criticised for a drama lesson and told it had been marked as a failing lesson. It is unusual to see drama going on in an Ofsted inspection for it is more risky than other lessons. However, this particular teacher had gone ahead with it in her classroom, although she usually did it in the hall but it was not available, because, 'it was good for them and I wanted the Ofsted team to see me working normally'. Her teaching is much admired by other teachers in her department: 'She's a great teacher—the bastards.'

The other teacher, Edith, was a temporary teacher in her first post. She had not been too worried by the thought of the inspection for she approved of inspections, as did Tracy. She was going to cope with inspection visits by pretending the inspector was not there. However in this particular lesson the inspector sat facing her about four yards away, 'invading my space.' People were angry at what they thought were unfair critical comments. 'She was seen eight times in three days and they only saw me five times and said nothing to me. It seems they were determined to go for the weakest link.' It was also noticed that the lead inspector had not conformed to the guidelines for lesson criticism as laid down by Ofsted for she had not informed these two teachers of their low gradings at the end of, either the lesson or the day on which these events occurred.

Staff gathered in support. At 5.10, six or more teachers moved from the first teacher's room to the second teacher's room to discuss the event and offer support and critique the inspectors' methods and judgements. One teacher was near to tears as she fumed at their unjust attack. At 5.20 one husband arrived to take one of them home and across the corridor the inspection team sat locked behind a closed door.

As two of the teachers go for a cup of tea to the staff room they walk past me looking grave and don't acknowledge me. The first teacher, Tracy, slowly walks out of the school burdened by many bags and flops into her elderly car and drives slowly out of the school. A few moments later the second teacher leaves, head lowered as she struggles with her bags following a few yards behind her husband who wearily fingers the car keys in his hand.

Back in the staff room people angrily comment 'it's wrong to focus on the temporary teacher. It's a waste of money.' The head teacher looks awful and has told the lead inspector what she thinks. She bangs the table angrily, with her fist, as she exclaims 'look what it's done to my staff.' 'Dip day' (known as the longest day of the inspector week) has become a self-fulfilling prophecy. I'm worried now that she might resign on Friday. She's pregnant, an agency teacher, has coped with the new yearly tests and worked hard. There was no indication that anyone was going to get the 'knock on the door' at 3.30.'

Suddenly the phone goes at 5.30. It's the first of the two teachers who wants to talk to the head teacher. I make a discreet exit and withdraw. The wind that was here on Sunday has returned if a little less strong and it is raining. Two other teachers are caught up in an altercation about something one of them said and another wants to criticise someone else for something she said to the inspector. At six o'clock we all leave. The head, the deputy and two other teachers leave, discussing how to redress the situation. It certainly has been a 'dip day'.

The collection of diverse data involving multiple behaviours practices and perspectives ensures that the researcher keeps his bias in check but it can also provide the empirical evidence to substantiate what appears to be common and stimulate an imperative to explain contrary behaviours between people and groups. The inclusion of this diverse material and the analytical work required to explain it legitimises, to some extent, the creative use of a researcher's empathy to represent the qualitative nature of the research site. However, alternative behaviours practices and perspectives are not always so clearly delineated as in an opposition.

Multiple behaviours, practices and perspectives

There is a temptation, when doing ethnography, to represent similar behaviours and practices as research findings, an implicit attempt to validate the research in quantitative terms particularly when alternative behaviours and perspectives are numerically less significant. The latter are then represented as being the exception to an identified phenomenon and therefore legitimating the common practice. A more sophisticated representation of this form of analysis is to use a typology, which includes specific number counts for each type (Pollard, 1994; Woods et al., 1996). The categorisations may be useful in understanding the extent of a range of reactions or behaviours but the numerical function, not only serves to justify the research in terms of quantifiable validity, but it depersonalises, objectifies and reifies the subjects of the research if the representation is left at this descriptive level. In real contexts individuals and groups do not always and consistently act according to the majority characterisation or the typology. In the inspection research teachers could be described as acting differently in a specific context. There were multiple reactions:

Carol felt the process unfair, her family relations were damaged, but, still lacking confidence, she 'mugged up', and *asserted herself*. Cloe (Trafflon) knew it was an impossible job, that teaching was complex, but she felt alone and in the end she *capitulated* and distanced herself from her past values, unlike Larry (Lowstate) who *appropriated* the process for his own enhancement. Graham, took it in his stride, 'I paced myself as I do when I am running'. He also *accepted* the system though he was not a supporter of an uncaring system of inspection, 'What will be will be'. Angelina thought the new inspection system divisive and didn't like it, but she 'was not in a position to alter it. I'm not going to waste my energy. I get on with doing what I'm good at, which is teaching children; it's them that count'. She was *ambivalent*: 'I'm not saying it's right and I'm not saying it's wrong, I'm saying it's a fact of life'. Laura had 'suffered in the past because I was against things so much. I was a bit of a rebel. Now I *go with the flow* and I am much happier. Inspections are opportunities to perform'.

These different reactions were put together as typologies as in an earlier analysis:

A. *Enhanced Teachers*. These teachers experience role conflict predominantly as dilemmas, and are enriched by their solutions to them. They feel able to employ their creative powers in their teaching and management. However, there are some ambivalent teachers here, who find both enrichment and tensions in the reforms.

B. *Compliant Teachers*. These experience a mixture of role dilemmas and tensions. Their creativity is deflected from teaching and towards devising strategies to cope. But there is wide variation among them, with some, for example, being positively conformist and seeing the social world as predominantly dilemmatic whereas others are more strategically compliant and/or more disturbed.

C. *Non-Compliant Teachers*. These also experience role tension, and to a somewhat worse degree since they are uncompromising in their values and in their practice.

D. *Diminished Teachers*. Role conflict for these is predominantly constraint in effect. They feel devalued and disillusioned, and are either 'leaving' the system or 'sinking' beneath it. (Woods et al. 1997 p. 50-51)

Specific teachers were then used as examples of sub categories of each of these types. We expressed clearly that this was a heuristic device, and that we were aware that these categories were one-dimensional and that it didn't fully represent each of the real people of the ethnography. However, it later seemed unsatisfactory. Consequently, in an attempt to provide an alternative to the 'typology' approach we later used 'coping strategies' as we considered that this conceptualisation provided a better representation of the fact that teachers acted in a contrasting manner at different times during these inspections. Coping strategies take into account reactions to situational constraints and the latter's relationship to wider social structures (Hargreaves, 1980)

> We found teacher responses here to be complex, and in some respects contradictory. At the same time as they were experiencing colonisation and deprofessionalisation the teachers were developing coping strategies. The latter, in themselves, contained apparently contrary behaviours. On the one hand, teachers *distanced* themselves from the Ofsted process in order to maintain their selves and professional identity. At the same time, they *engaged* extensively with the process in order to satisfy the corporate pressures and their faith and commitment to work. These behaviours were generally exhibited simultaneously by the majority of the teachers although within these categories teachers positioned themselves differently.   (ibid. p. 141)

Coping strategies are more flexible in dealing with diverse responses and typifications. They are more capable of entertaining the possibility of multiple actions in the face of an event that causes an individual to act. The use of immersion by ethnographers to portray a comprehensive representation of actors and contexts should lead to a higher level of analysis than descriptive typologies to account for contrary behaviours and practices of both individuals and groups across types.

Contradictory behaviours, practices and perspectives

Acting differently according to the context—multiple behaviours practices and perspectives—may also be interpreted as acting in a contradictory manner. This might be contradictory in terms of what people have articulated and expressed verbally about their values and beliefs, for example, not letting the children 'play' when inspectors were around. They may also behave in a contradictory manner from one week to the next. The use of a contradictory lens to gather data reveals the paradoxes of lived realities. Tracy, the teacher criticised for her drama lesson, supported inspections, 'I think they are a good thing, they keep schools on their toes. It's also good for everybody to see the good things in a school, to publicise it'. Her other lessons were considered satisfactory and although her overall view of inspections didn't change, her assessment drew out the negative processes of this inspection system:

> I was in tears; it was terrible. The atmosphere, passing them and seeing them, coming in here. I didn't want to come back to school; it was not pleasant. I wish they could do it another way, perhaps to come in informally and see how we're doing.

Her experience contradicted her expectations and this created a credibility gap in terms of Ofsted's legitimacy as well as alienating her.

A further contradiction concerning the legitimacy of Ofsted's assessment was discovered by maintaining contact with the school after the Ofsted inspection. Rose was commended in the Ofsted inspection and then criticised in a later Local Education Authority (LEA) inspection which used Ofsted's criteria and as a result of that criticism, the management of the school suggested she went on an educational revision course. 'She is not particularly happy about it' (Keith). She refused to be interviewed after the LEA inspection. Contradictions in the process of the inspection system devalue its effects and the support it wanted to gain from teachers.

Another flaw in the inspectorial process was uncovered when one teacher received contradictory treatment. Simca, a new teacher, received a good assessment but the actual inspection report included her in a 'failing' department:

> I was just pissed off because one of the inspectors had taken me aside and told me that 'your teaching approach is right', but the actual written report criticised the department as a whole. Now there is now going to be training for all our department and it has made me start to question my teaching methods and my philosophy.

Diane noted another contradiction within the Ofsted process:

When I assess my own failings or do it with somebody local, I can do something to get them right and I can then compare my next effort with my previous effort, and I can evaluate whether I am getting better or not? But they've taken a snapshot of me, and they won't be coming back to find out if the next time if I do it any better, so I am left with the feeling that I am a failure.

Hit and run inspections like Ofsted do not, she argues, present a rational approach to improve teachers' performance. Abstract systems such as audit accountability (Power 1994) need to gain the trust of those on whom they operate. It could be argued that this means attending to a rational process that includes the teacher in a developmental framework.

An example of institutional meso practices containing contradictions is the experience of Rita, a deputy head who was worried that the inspection would be an opportunity for someone to damage the corporate image of the school by complaining about some staff bullying:

Some are almost talking in terms of using the inspection as a vehicle to 'blow the whistle' on the person who's been upsetting them, and I am very frightened, that that's going to happen, because I don't want that to surface, certainly not during an Ofsted inspection.

She found herself having to cover up poor managerial practice for the sake of the school's image in the educational 'market place'. This was perverse contradictory behaviour for she also suffered from the bullying, but the market climate within education in England at this time precluded 'blowing the whistle' on the perpetrator. Schools had to ensure that they presented a unified image to an examining process that might have seen them get a 'failing' report and therefore institutional flaws were covered up. From this contradiction, analysis relating to the effectiveness of a market system in Education was reviewed in the final representation.

Tracy, Rose Simca, Diane and Rita have had to face up to contradictions, which not only distress them and cause them to reconsider reconstructing their teaching identity, but they also reveal contradictions at the heart of some of the inspection's values and processes. Private troubles are public issues (Mills, 1959) and the exposure of contradictions at the micro empirical level reflect contradictions in meso and macro structures.

When Grace, a deputy head, had an argument with one of her friends in her department, resulting in severed relations between them for a few weeks, this was seen as contradictory behaviour by the other teacher:

> She really shouted at me and she said 'I don't want to talk about it' and she just walked away and I just got really upset and screamed and shouted and said 'for God's sake'. I think I was really shocked and I resented it because I felt I had completed my preparation even though she had criticised me for not doing so. But passions were rising so high because everyone was trying to make everything so perfect.

This contradictory behaviour served as an indicator of the tension and stress of maintaining 'persona of perfection' (Hargreaves, 1994).

Lucy's story of a breakdown in her relationship with her head teacher shows clearly the effect of the inspection on the latter. The head teacher telephoned her while she was absent attending to her daughter in hospital to tell her she would not be paid during her absence:

> One of the reasons why I decided to come here was her humanity. She wasn't the sort to be distant and aloof. She was usually understanding and sympathetic. I don't think she would have reacted in that way before the inspection. I think it's affected her judgement.

However, her head teacher later regretted her actions. Lucy's head teacher

> was very apologetic and I know that she got very upset herself and said, 'I didn't mean it that way and I've been very thoughtless', but, the damage had been done in terms of management creditability.

The pressures on teachers with a managerial role to focus on systems rather than people were undermining the human relationships among the staff that cemented the collaborative culture that was typical of this school. Thus, Toni's role as deputy head and leading curriculum co-ordinator led her to put pressure on others and regretting it, even though she felt it was unavoidable. She photocopied some more statistics for co-ordinators to consider a week prior to the inspection, and one particular teacher, whom she liked and worked well with, reacted particularly emotionally, as Toni bitterly observes:

Tears came to her eyes, and I thought 'Oh God, I've done it again!' It's my management role, I've got no choice, I appreciate the timing is bad but I couldn't do anything about it. I thought I was actually being quite helpful by going away at 7.30 in the morning and photocopying these bits of paper. I totally realise her reaction wasn't to do with me. It was to do with feeling very, very worried and concerned about presenting the stuff to inspectors. What I'm saying is that the end result of me trying to be helpful and efficient and giving teachers more information, was to make somebody feel really, really upset and say 'I know I'm going to make a mess of this'.

Contradictory behaviours exist within people as well and recording these can illustrate the amount of identity work (Snow and Anderson 1987) that goes on when people become anxious or they are faced with challenges to their 'substantial selves' (Nias, 1989) as Cloe indicates:

I still am worried; I haven't found me yet. I haven't found myself because I do in fact care. I don't feel that I'm working *with* the children any more, I'm working *at* the children but it's not a very pleasant experience. You feel responsible for every part of the school, whether you had anything to do with it or not but at the same time I feel alienated from it all, divorced from it all. Does that make sense? No it doesn't really.

Contradictions between values and practice are indicative of unequal power relations and resolutions indicate coping strategies:

I don't think the focus is constructive at all, I'm very suspicious of it but if putting computer written labels all over the classroom will keep somebody happy, I'll do it. I see it as like playing a game.   (Amy)

Teachers begin to develop a series of separate situational contradictory identities. Practice became contrived; teachers played the inspectors at their own game. Amy, who was commended by the inspectors, began to think:

'He isn't bloody coming, he's late'. I was conscious that this lesson was good and he wasn't watching it. So I extended it and he arrived a few minutes later, It was a pure performance for him. It wasn't necessary for the children but I was conscious that I was being judged and assessed.

Goffman (1959) has written of how one

> 'presents oneself' in order to control the conduct of others, especially their responsive treatment of him (sic) ... This control is achieved largely by influencing the definition of the situation which the others come to formulate, and he can influence this definition by expressing himself in such a way as to give them the kind of impression that will lead them to act voluntarily in accordance with his own plan.　　(Ibid. pp. 15-16)

Carol found the contradictions between her professional beliefs and the expectations of Ofsted difficult to resolve. For example, Ofsted believed that you could determine programme of work in a classroom a year in advance. Carol argued that the pace and development of the children concerned must, to some extent, determine the curriculum:

> I've always had a structure but I've always worked on what the kids have got interested in and involved in. I've always drawn from the children and I've always gone off at tangents if it's got really interesting. So I'm finding it difficult now. We're doing a project on shape at the moment and the plan was to look at a different shape each week but the kids got so wrapped up in it that we were doing circles for about 3 weeks. We're still doing triangles now and they're so enthusiastic about it that it seems pointless to actually suddenly decide artificially to move on to squares as the plans demand.

However, this situation did not result in Carol either becoming deprofessionalised or reprofessionalised, but both (Troman, 1997). Her solution was to hop between the discourses. She was resentful as well as being resigned and amenable. Nevertheless she maintained professional responsiveness and she kept in touch with her values. Her professional identity as a member of a valued and recognised professional structure had been damaged by the marginalisation of that structure. The meso structure of professional knowledge and educational values, which assisted her construction of identity, had been removed. Her 'sense of place', in terms of educational values had been removed.

So she attempted to regain a sense of place by drawing on her own humanity for the people she worked with and in order to do this at times she engaged with them in implementing a new programme. At the same time she maintained as many links to her 'substantial self' (Nias, 1989), that presented themselves. She did not lose her past but she did lose control over her present. She may never be able to 'go back' but she can draw on the past again, if along with others, she is able to re-establish 'place' as a determinant of identity and professionalism.

At present Carol is living a fragmented professional life hopping between discourses and straddling them. She contrasts the discourses of technicisation and value based working practices and at the same time she engages with the conflicts and contradictions within both discourses (for a fuller account see Jeffrey, 1999)

The search for contradictions is rewarded by the discovery of the paradoxes and dilemmas of people's lives and at the same time the discoveries often reflect the contradictions at the heart of macro and meso structures.

Conclusion

Having employed oppositional and multiple behaviours as well as contradictory data collection lenses to interpret the inspection research we were left with the task of surmising an explanation as to how these inspectors and teachers managed the competing imperatives (Alexander, 1995) of their situation. We invoked discourse theory:

Teachers have *multi-faceted*, rather than fragmented, selves, and they demonstrate considerable skill at developing and employing strategies first situations. This apparent strategical switching is best explained, we argue, through the concept of 'positioning'.

> In addition each person brings to any episode of collaborative constitution of the world in this or that way, their accumulated personal history—their sense of themselves not only as they were positioned in the present moment but also of themselves as persons who can or cannot be positioned in that way, i.e. as one who is located in certain ways within the social and moral order, who is known to act and feel in certain ways, whose life is explicable within known story lines.
>
> (Davies and Harre 1984 p 342)

Teachers position themselves among a number of different discourses such as 'child centredness', 'corporate responsibility', or 'managerialism' according to their own professional biographies. To our teachers, inspectors' actions, seem positioned within one discourse, that of managerialism, but the inspectors saw themselves as positioned in terms of Government objectives (Woods and Jeffrey 1998). So we looked for a theory that could cater for the oppositional, multiple and contradictory data we collected.

It has been suggested that the collection of data from any ethnographic site which includes amongst the researcher's 'lenses' oppositional, multiple and contradictory behaviours practices and perspectives will enhance an ethnography by:

- Encouraging the researcher to explain the contrary findings;
- Assist the researcher in making the 'familiar strange';
- Provide legitimate space for the inclusion of researcher empathy;
- Uncover the paradoxical and dilemmatic nature of lived reality; and
- Reveal the often inherent contradictory characteristics of a broader social structures and practices.

As a result of using these particular lenses explicitly, the complexities of lived reality are illuminated and explained by descriptive explanations. The distinctiveness of theories is not their theoretical character but he explicitness and coherence of the models employed and the rigour of the data collection analysis (Hammersley 1992).

Chapter 5

The deceptive imagination and ethnographic writing

Dennis Beach

Introduction

This chapter has been developed from an earlier piece of work (Beach, 2002) that examined aspects of what I termed there as a post-modern celebration in experimental writing in ethnography has turned reflexivity towards ethnographic authorship, which is taken as fully relativistic in the post-modern moment, even though the admission of such a depth of relativistic interdependency can lead to Nihilism and not just to the more hoped for awakening of questions about the position of ethnographic representation in a creative moment of indeterminacy and response to a criticism of traditional writing forms based on a recognition of how their politics of 'content of form' worked in favour of various kinds of domination and a West is best philosophy (see also e.g. Tyler, 1987; Watson, 1987; Lather, 1991; Denzin, 2000; Tedlock, 2000; Kanepalli Kanth, 1999). This chapter has been revisited and reworked a little for the present collection in order to, as Clough (2000) also expresses it, refocus the ethnographic intention with the experimental moment, which was to support a deconstruction and rethinking of the philosophy of presence in ethnography, in order to contribute to the possibilities for social and cultural critique (Clifford and Marcus (eds), 1986; Marcus and Fischer, 1986; Marcus, 1998; Denzin, 2000; Tedlock, 2000; Beach, 2003). It does this by considering how one piece of critical, experimental writing in the social sciences has, in an empirically researched situation, been said by readers of it to have convinced them of its true meaning.

This piece of writing is a critically reflexive text written by Michael Mulkay on the history of the relationship of the human and natural sciences (Mulkay, 1989 in Mulkay, 1991). It is ethnographic in a sense described by Atkinson (1990), as it communicates a message about an aspect of the anthropological junctures of human culture by the use of synecdochical tropes (see also Marcus and Fischer, 1986) and is critically reflexive in the sense expressed in Bleakley (2000, p. 28), as it shows an aesthetic sensitivity to competing positions and difference by acting from within an ethical standpoint that respects the tolerance of difference and ambiguity and the negotiation of explanatory power.

Mulkay's text is an evocative piece of creative writing which includes an introduction sequence about the dilemma of understanding science post critical/reflexive or literary turn (be this from the outside or the inside), an expressionistic love-story, a satirical play on a couple of ways of reading this story, a reflection over the contributions and exclusions of these texts and a self-ironising monologue around the achievements of a researcher-author, which helps return thinking to the originally considered problem. It has been read by me and used in teaching about social science methods on qualitative methods courses at three different levels (initial teacher education, in-service training and on a PhD course), with all in all forty-seven students. In these contexts it has been read, discussed and (re-)presented in *conversational inter-views* (Kvale, 1996) by reader-analysts in relation to the textual construction and main messages 'recognised in' or 'constructed from' the text.

The love story is expressed by the author and the students reading the text as being the main piece, an idea that is also backed up by its central position in the chapter in question and references to it in other parts. This text-piece is also allegorical. That is, it is a figurative representation in which something is presented through indirect story telling. This presence of allegory tended to form the main focus of the discussions between the other reader analysts and myself that have formed the main cornerstone of the empirical data for the present chapter. The love story is written in the following way:

A Moving Story of Love and Bondage[1]

She had never seen anyone like him before. In the golden glow of the enlightenment his very being shone like a God. Indeed the rumour was that he had banished God to a backroom in the universe and was going to use Newton's Laws to run the whole thing himself. He was the master she had been longing for. She knew, from that very moment, that she was meant to be his slave and that her life was destined to be intimately intertwined with his.

She knew of course that she was unworthy of him. She would never be able to acquire his quality of mind, his economy and precision of language, or his ... will to conquer. That was not her nature. Her concern was with people not things. Her task ... was to care for their needs and to help them through their troubles. But she believed in her ... innocence, she could imitate him well enough to become his ... partner in his struggle to

---

1. I world like to thank Professor Michael Mulkay for his permission to use and reproduce *The Moving Story of Love and Bondage* from Mulkay (1989).

improve mans lot through the pursuit of knowledge. She would ... teach herself to think, speak and act as he did. He would become her model in all things ... As time went by she saw his achievements multiply. As the natural world came increasingly under his control, she strove to apply his techniques to her own humble realm of human affairs. Of course, he took little notice of her modest labours and, when their fruits were brought to his attention, he derided them as worthless, woman's things. But she was not discouraged. Indeed her ardour was inflamed by his effortless superiority and she tried even harder to subdue the human world as he had taken command of all that was not human.

The decades passed by and then turned into centuries. The first strands of gray could now be seen in her once lustrous hair and the shine in her eyes was less brilliant. She felt that she had done all that could be expected of her, but still their union seemed no closer. She was sure that her spirit was tuned to his. But he did not seem to return her feelings. She sometimes suspected that he said cruel things about her when he was closeted with his friends. Most revealing, and hurtful, of all, he pointedly refused to allow her to attend the yearly festival of the Nobel Ceremonies when all that was great and good was praised and rewarded.

Slowly, imperceptibly at first (but with growing momentum) she began to have doubts about the man she had loved and admired ... How could he be so ... unmoved by her devotion? Did he still have those fine qualities which had touched her heart all those years ago? Had she ever properly understood him? She began to wonder whether the pledge she had made in her youth had been based on an illusion. If so, it might not be too late to start again. But first she must find out the truth. Her new quest, she decided, would be to apply his methods of understanding, as well as she could, to discovering what sort of a person he really was ... She already knew many of his writings, of course. But he never stopped producing more and the range of his knowledge increased at a daunting speed. Although she read and re-read, and re-read and re-read, she felt that the man she was searching for was hidden from view behind the elegant neutrality of his written texts. In addition, she was deeply worried by the texts themselves. How had she ever been impressed by this simplistic, yet cumbersome, language and by his manipulative way of relating to the world? She began to talk to those who knew him well. They spoke of him with great admiration. But, she felt, to be praised in this unreserved fashion by industrialists, entrepreneurs, politicians and the military, was in itself a kind of implicit condemnation. Anyway, she got a strong impression that there was an undercurrent of fear (and) that their professions of confidence in the man she loved (or was it the man she had loved?) were underlain by a nagging suspicion that he no-longer knew what he, or they, were doing and that the world they had raped together was now going to pay them back in kind.

She was shocked by her own thoughts. She had never seen it like this before, but somehow 'rape' now seemed appropriate. His basic assumption was, she realised, that knowledge was the same thing as control; and the basic assumption of his companions seemed to be that knowledge gave you the right to control, that is, to dominate, exploit and subjugate for your own ends. The 'god' of her youth was beginning to look, as she approached middle-age, more like a 'devil'. It was time she decided, to go and talk to the man himself.

On her first visit, he was quite charming ... and invited her to pursue any line of inquiry that she wished. 'I have nothing to hide' he insisted with a laugh. However, he wouldn't allow her to tape-record a discussion which 'might touch upon delicate political issues'. She noted down the general gist of his responses: 'Not my fault if things go wrong *out there*. Soon have all basic answers. Cheap, inexhaustible energy just around the corner. Solve problem of Global overheating immediately. Seal up ozone layer with self-reproducing micro-organisms designed to reflect harmful rays. Train aquatic mammals and use them to cleanse oceans. More money needed for research. Just a bit more time to achieve perfect unity of knowledge. Nearly there already. Three down, one to go. Once we've got that, control whole system. Better life for all—as long as they do what they're told.'

This monologue didn't exactly rekindle her love for him. But maybe he ... did have the ability to take everything under his control and make it run perfectly, in due course. Yet what did it mean to make it run 'perfectly'? And in whose interests would control be exercised ... She put these questions to him. She was distressed and shocked by his reply, which was ... that this was none of his business. She was the one, he pointed out, who dealt with people. It was up to her to develop her own 'perfect unity of knowledge' that could be used to control the social world in the same way that he would soon have total mastery over the physical and biological domains.'When you have achieved this' he said,'I will welcome you into my dwelling and we will at last join together to create a perfect, ordered world for all human kind.'

At these words she turned in horror from him and ran out of his world. She had finally come to realise that the man she had loved was emotionally, morally and even intellectually deformed. He was, she now knew, unable to see the world from another's point of view; unable to understand that there could be no perfect unity in the realm of human affairs because the social world was not unitary, but multiple. She saw for the first time that her fragmentary and distorted conception of social life, her concern with its concrete, ever-changing particulars, were not signs of her failure, as she had always believed, but evidence of her success.

Suddenly she felt free as if an intolerable burden had been lifted from her mind. The cost of learning the truth had been great ... Her youth had been sacrificed to an illusion. (But) now ... a middle-aged woman adrift in a sick and dying culture ... she was for the first time able to think for herself and to begin to create her own language; which would be a language, not of domination and control ... but of imagination and freedom.   (from Mulkay, 1991: 23-25)

Commentary I. (Re)collections

The beginning of Mulkay's poem includes the following: *She had never seen anyone like him before ... He was the master she had been longing for. She knew ... that she was meant to be his slave and (that) her life was destined to be intimately intertwined with his ...* This *opens* the first part of a story which, as is indicated earlier, is positioned between an introductory monologue on what this story is meant to speak to (i.e. the dilemma of *understanding* science and the historical relationship between the social and natural sciences) and a satirical *play* in which this dilemma and the logic of the response in the story are explored.

The positioning of the story is important for its effects, I will suggest later, as is the possession of both a verisimilitude (the semblance of reality in dramatic or non-dramatic fiction) and a vraisemblance (a double truth) in both it and in the retrospective satire and self-ironising closing monolog that follow it. According to the conversations I have had with other reader-analysts, these are the things which together allow for a textual hyperbole in the work, in which what is actually written in the words of a piece of fictional prose about love and a gender identity struggle, become convincing *toward another* (non-fictional) *object* through the way in which they help to create imagined relations toward a world beyond the story's own words and the previous experiences and knowledge of the audience.

Inventive of interpretation (hyperbole) is an aim but no easy literary task in ethnography (see also Atkinson, 1990; Van Maanen, 1988, 1995 and Tedlock, 2000). However, it seems to be *managed* in the text by Mulkay, I and the other reader-analysts felt, through the construction and use of a number of specific tropes, which each play on the civilisational ethos of gender relations in societies like ours. For instance, there is a direct reference to the servitude of woman to man (which has been read to *play on* the received understanding of the relations of language and social science to natural sciences by all bar two of the readers), passing reference to the dominance of the male way and masculine virtue (which has been read to play on the generally acknowledged *common sense and ideological* understandings of the superiority of scientific knowledge over intuition and paradigmatic/rational over connotative/intuitive knowledge in modernity by all bar two of the readers), an inference toward the female concern for (social) relationships and feminine virtue (which has been read to play on the acknowledged objects of *social* rather than natural science by all bar two of the readers) and a strong attraction by the woman in the story toward the man, which although it doesn't last, may be said to deepen initially. This has been recognised by all of the readers, all of whom have read it as playing firstly on the movement in social science towards logical positivism, then the development of its hegemony and finally the growth of reactions against it in critical theory, feminism, post-structuralism and post-colonial and ethnic theory.

The weakening of the attraction which the woman in the story feels for the man was understood as a key feature by all the readers, according to conversation data on this point, that was felt to be brought about initially by the identification of a gut-feeling of rejection or non-belonging by the woman, a feeling in other words, that was followed by her beginning to question firstly the recognition and reciprocation of her love and secondly the values which she had attributed to him and to which she at least thought she had previously been attracted. This critical juxtaposition of source materials (including emotional knowledge and sensual evidence); which is a very ethnographic characteristic; in other words brought the woman in the story to begin to search further (i.e. became a motor in her continuing venture) and contrast things like—*She knew she was unworthy of him (but she would try) to teach herself to think speak and act as he did (and) He* *would become her model in all things (as she) strove to apply his techniques to her humble realm ... —*with other issues. First the doubt, *Was this the man she had loved ... or (only) thought she had loved.* And then the self-disparagement: *How could she have been attracted by his clumsy language ...*

Commentary II. Ethnographic suggestions

The ideas expressed by the reader-analysts concerning the use of juxtaposition and its effects were described in interviews as essentially ethnographic by the course participants and as suggesting that Mulkay's 'Moving Story' shows several qualities of synedoche and verisimilitude that hint at one of the ways in which ethnographic writers can use common knowledge and shared frames of experience when writing for a known audience in order to shake them and disturb their consciousness. That is, how texts can gain their meaning from the *specifically situated work* of such elements (see also Barthes, 1977; Beach, 1995, ch. 2). This reflexive juxtaposition of opposites and parallel comparisons is also a common feature in critical, post-structural and feminist writing in the social sciences (see also Tedlock, 2000), making these into very valuable source materials for inspiration in ethnographic writing.

These traditions, as Mulkay does, often use juxtaposition to play on our emotions through troubling and contrasting the common/dominant cultural myth themes of Western civilisation. In Mulkay's story there was for instance a love at first sight description celebrating the patriarchal perspective of the subordination of woman to man in his image and valorising the (religious) heterosexuality myth of the attraction of gendered opposites. These common myth themes of Western (and also some other) civilisations clash with the lived reality of the reader subjects, as the sanctity of such attractions and relations of soft femininity and dominant manliness as naturally attracted opposites and as reciprocal qualities within two science traditions under modernity are constantly troubled and transcended in real life, through the way they break against post-modern interrogations of the same and first hand emotional experience. In ways also hinted at in Aristotle's Poetics regarding how idealised characters always possess qualities which allow the probable to take precedence over what is otherwise only (a weak) possibility, in the context provided for and by the story *understandings* change character as the conventions of modernity are first subtly challenged and then vanquished.

The juxtaposition of opposites is something which is expressed as essential in deepening understandings of culture in both ethnographic reading and writing—according to authors as different as Hammersely (1992) and Atkinson (1990) on the one hand, Tyler (1987), Clifford (1986), van Maanen (1988, 1995) and Tedlock (2000) on the other and Willis (1977, 1999, 2000), Grossberg, (1996) and Alvesson and Deetz (2000) on a third. Through it a deepening of awareness is said to be possible (together with a form of self-understanding) that derives from something more than just an element of self-reflection. Indeed, rather than being formed in self-reflection, the juxtaposition of opposites is suggested to be more in line with Schopenhauer's critique of the same, in which in his terms we always risk losing ourselves in the bottomless void of (our own) personality, by floundering in the unfathomable depths of the self and a bottomless void of searching for real-knowledge about a non-real subject (also Bleakley, 2000). Indeed according to the Ph.D. reader-analysts' statements, juxtaposition is more in tune with Bhaktins notion of the carnivalesque, where a variety of often conflicting positions are displayed and where differences are celebrated and new ideas formed in a reverie of representations (Bleakley, 2000). The reverie of representations was suggested in conversations to be another key ethnographic trait that is sometimes termed polyphony and sometimes termed experimentation.

The reader-analysts pointed out that a number of (perhaps unexpected) possibilities emerge for the woman because of its carnivalesque qualities of juxtaposition and experimentation. For instance, it is through the juxtaposition of opposites that the woman first kindles thoughts of disaffection, which then deepen and finally contribute to the formation of a new quest in which she vows to begin to unveil her former heart-throbs true characteristics, but which then even leads her to question the very foundations upon which all expressions of love and admiration are actually based.[2] Furthermore, in this movement the woman also came to see that the man intended to use her in his project of world domination, where she would be seen by him to measure up to his standards, or to fail them. And it was at this point that she turned and ran out of his world as she came for the first time to see that her fragmentary

---

2. With a basis in her new realisations the woman in the story decided to learn more about the man she loved and set off to interview him and some of those who professed to be his friends. In this process (interviewing is seen in process terms, not the mining of facts from the head of another: see also Kvale, 1995), and as her conversations with him and about him grew, the woman became increasingly aware of the basically warped nature of the man and that he was and always had been incapable of seeing the world from another's point of view, that he was disinterested in and incapable of understanding himself and his relationship to the world and was (therefore) incapable of accepting responsibility for his own actions. He was, she realised, not the lover she had hoped and that rather than being the caring, kindly father figure toward the world he often claimed to be, he was instead a monster who sought to conquer it, dominate it and subjugate other human kind to his own ends.

and disordered conception of social life were not signs of her failure, as he had made her believe, but evidence of her success to resist total objectification in a singular, dominant class interest. These outcomes are expressed by three of the Ph.D. readers to liken the processes and effects of immanent criticism in critical theory, where an ideal concept is first constructed and then used as a tool of critical re-analysis with which to confront a situation to which it is meant to relate (see also Alvesson and Deetz, 2000).

However critical theory was not the only (or even the main) common research paradigm or tradition recognised in the text-work by Mulkay by the reader analysts, who rather more often tended to equate the approach to truth taken in Mulkay's work to post-modern, dialogical research. This is reflected in the social and (inter-)textual constructions of reality in the text according to the reader analysts, its ending a new beginning and the strength claimed on behalf of uncertainty, tentativity and feelings in this new beginning (see also Lather, 2000), as opposed to certainty and the power of a universal and objective truth (see also Kanepalli Kanth, 1999). This post-modern turn in the story, according to my own reading and about half of the comments from other readers was also suggested to have always been an ever-present, immanent and repressed side of the woman's identity waiting to be let out

Commentary III. Illusion, imagination and the power of Pseudos with/in ethnography

In the above section I have presented my and also the reader-analysts' comments on Mulkay's love story as very positive (at times almost revering), by almost seeming to support the idea that this story poetically *reveals* something to us by evoking realist images of an imaginary presence in a way that makes otherwise dense and difficult historical and political relations within the history of science more *transparent* and easily grasped. Indeed, we may be seen to say even, that the text is giving voice to something which would otherwise remain silent of an oppressed or marginalised party in the history of science on the one hand and heterosexual *partnerships* on the other. However, these 'positive readings' belie other quite different possibilities, particularly as I actually have a sense that although the story almost feels as if it is reflecting real relations in the histories mentioned, this sense is inevitably constructed in an interplay between the words of the text and sensations which the text awakens through its classically ethnographic use of vivid images in place of generalities and abstractions to link the authors fantasy to the reader's imagination.

Verisimilitude and metonymy (i.e. the use of vivid images for generalities and abstractions)—together with synedoche and vraisemblance—are key rhetorical elements in ethnogrraphy, and their presence in (and in the present case suggested domination of) the production-promotion of a particular awareness, might be of significance even when it comes to understanding how ethnographic messages are more generally formed. Such an argument supports Barthes (1977), Atkinson (1990) and Tedlock (2000) at least, who all assert that it is such elements of rhetoric that interplay with/in a given readerly context to create the particular messages of a text. However, it must still be pointed out that in this process it is, actually, through the power of the imagination and past experiences, that what is represented in one context seems to be like something else in another one and means that to call Mulkay's text, and texts like it, realistic (or even realist fiction), in the way one may when revering what can appear to be revelations in them, is a very misleading distortion (Tedlock, 2000). And it is very clear that this is so! Because *neither* the actual story of the love relationship written on directly *nor* the images of a history of science and the workings of a gender regime to which it evocatively relates, are realistically true in the conventional sense of that term. In fact, however persuasive the text may feel, it really works in Genosko's terms as *a Nietzshean reverie on the power of Pseudos* (Genosko, 1994: 28) rather than through its *realism*. It convinces us more as a fable than by direct referencing, in other words, at a point where truth and fiction merge with/in a textual politics, where the possibilities of inter-textuality limit the variety of themes that a text may touch upon, on the basis of how that text coalesces with feelings and prior knowledge.

On the other hand, the point with the present text is not to claim that Mulkay's story is either deliberately enlightening and envisioning or deliberately false and misleading. Rather, all that is being suggested is that *the story is*. That is, that it exists as a text which has been crafted in the specific sense that Mulkay has put a good deal of imagination into the use of a set of fairly standard myth themes and characters, such that what they describe can be understood by (some) readers in terms of a specific criticism to which the author intends them to become related. Yet at the same time as this is accepted, my view on the issue of inter-textuality in the work has to be re-angled, as Mulkay's text itself can now be considered as impressionistic (in style) in its references toward a standard love-affair (and sexual attraction) myth theme of Western civilisation/culture, within a context where the author has gone to some lengths to encourage specific recollections of knowledge (and assumptions) about a second context. This gives the story something of an *expressionistic* character where, in the poetic links between the impressionist love story and the understanding it helps to create, some inner feelings are given greater voice than others in the (re-)framing of the *truth* of a particular story. This means that whilst on the one hand the text is able to appear 'within the true' (see Rabinow, 1986) with respect to a life history as it could have happened, on the other it also makes inferences about a world beyond this content, to thus constitute a lens which allows us to see this aspect of the world in a particular (and perhaps different/unconventional way) way. The story represents a theory, in other words, in the critical sense of the term, a recognition also made by several of the PhD reader-analysts of the text. One motivation for this (kind of) textuality politics can be summed up as follows:

> Both science and literature are aspects of Textuality. Science is a form of Textuality that is based on the assumption that there is a single coherent factual world which can be accurately and consistently represented by the application of a constant method, and to a considerable degree controlled by the textual producer. Literature is another form of Textuality, the basic premise of which is that there are many potential worlds of meaning that can be imaginatively entered into and celebrated, in ways which are constantly changing, to give richness and value to human experience. Both these forms of Textuality furnish us with the means of relating to the world and of giving expression to that world ... Society can be read for regularity, order, coherence and control according to the scientific format. Or it can be read for disorder, diversity, incommensurability and so on, through the production of openly creative texts.
>
> (Mulkay, 1991, p. 27-28)

Another motivation is as follows:

> Although modern culture has for the most part standardised on the scientific method as the preferred way to obtain and validate knowledge, no such agreement exists among the traditional societies that are evolving into post-colonial cultures. From a modernist perspective, in which the efficacy of scientific technology is unquestioned, alternative ways of thinking can look quaint or whimsical. Assuming the universal seriousness of human attempts to understand self and world, however, this dismissive sort of judgement risks missing an important

philosophical point: any way of knowing is intimately bound up with ones meta-physical understanding of the nature of the world and ones existence in it. Thus, a challenge to *what* one knows *and how* one knows is not necessarily *just* (sic.) addressing the issue of whether a claim about an alleged fact is true, but can also be constructed as a challenge to ones deepest beliefs. This is a point of no small significance for post-colonial thought, which deals in part with the effects of precisely such challenges.

(Moore and Bruder, 1996, p.636)

The above two quotes may help to suggest that authors such as Mulkay are wild post-modernists who value variety and will uphold the potential for dissensus even within and toward their own writing, in order to interrupt conventional understandings and open up new possible realms of meaning. However, in the present example, we also have a situation where a particular and very restricted set of outcomes have been fairly consistently reproduced at individual levels, so perhaps the suggestion for ethnographic writing can be best expressed as follows. That by virtue of the specific relations between its classifications and its framing arrangements within an anticipated context, Mulkay's text is one which makes its readers into critical and creative thinkers and doers of social and human science as they read it, with a focus and *intentionality* which is preconceived by the writer himself. This would also support an idea advanced in the words of one of the reader-analysts of the text, that it is 'by virtue of an enticing play of words on emotions, knowledge and human sensibilities', that the author has been able to capture the imagination of a group of readers 'and help them toward a particular understanding in relation to a specific set of issues and relations which were never directly *spoken on* or written about'.

There are two quite different implications nested in the above with respect to ethnographic writing more generally in my view. The first of these is a rather idealistic or romantic suggestion that ethnographic writing should aim to encourage its readers to become co-ethnographers of the elements of culture described in a piece of work whilst reading and reflecting on it. This idealisation is often deeply romanticised in writings about ethnographic reflexivity (Marcus and Fischer, 1986; Tyler, 1987; Marcus, 1998; Tedlock, 2000). The second idea is perhaps more cynical and suggests that because the example text has a very clear readership of which its author is aware, with clear readerly limits which he (first) deliberately stretches and then plays with (but does not try to over-reach), the author is very much aware of how a rhetorical force can sweep hold of understanding and capture the imagination of readers, and that he tries to use this to the full. This is again in line with Atkinson's suggestions about ethnographic writing being primarily convincing through its use of rhetoric (Atkinson, 1990; Hammersley, 1992; Tedlock, 2000).

The idea that the author may be steering the readers in the above way is at least partially confirmed later in the chapter from which the love story is taken, in the satirical play which follows it and which informs us on how the story can (and I feel Mulkay means should) be read, which also suggests two further points. The first is that readers are always *positioned readers* in relation to any story (partly by the art of the author, partly by their experiences and personalities) and that a story is not likely to mean the same thing to differently positioned readers. For instance the present text wouldn't mean the same thing to a 16th century astronomer, a 20th century literary critic or a post-modern philosopher of science. Nor would it likely mean the same if told to a South African bushman, an interface designer, an architect, or a computer engineer. The second suggestion is that a student of social science research methods can be positioned by an author to receive a story in particular ways.

Together the two suggestions above signify the importance of knowledge of audience, but they also provide a link between the two previous ideas about what ethnographic writing (and writers) aim to do with, to or for their readers, as reflecting these ideas against the two suggestions implies that making the reader into a positioned ethnographer of a text can now be seen as a political project of first selecting and targeting and then preparing ones audience as desired, by the use of specifically identified form of *conversational* politics (Tedlock, 2000). This brings us even to a third point, conversational texts can be written to articulate meaning in critical ethnography, where rather than illustrating fixed mental representations of the world texts (should be set out to) challenge such representations. This is important to understand in relation to writing (and reading ethnography) and speaks directly to the ease with which digressions may be inserted into prose, so as to afford fiction a non-fictional freedom that challenges pre-figured meanings by engaging with and disturbing them so that enlightenment (or revelation) and deception are able to merge.

However, this is an idea that introduces a potentially more negative understanding of Mulkay's writing politics and *story*, as it suggests that this story may actually only ensnare, enrapture or seduce us to believe in his own theory of science, by toying with our emotions and imagination. This idea gives yet another angle on rhetorical art (and allegory) to the two forms of positive imagery spoken of previously, where I suggested the possibility of a text having a politics of form which is (firstly) either revealing something important to a reader or (secondly) inviting her/him to be a co-doer of social science when reading a text, because of the way it is written. This new angle is given in that this *art* can now be seen as something which deliberately aims to fix us in the grip of a view of an aspect of the world which an author sees as important, by instilling us in a pseudo reality for which we are also subconsciously prepared by her/him. That is, the text makes us see what actually isn't (objectively) there with an enthusiasm which increases our scope to grasp things that we would never otherwise wholly perceive.

I put this idea to the other reader-analysts of the text, who all agreed that such could be the case and that thus a rhetorical and allegorical text actually seduces us with a kind of hypnotic power, as in reading it, we unexpectedly become aware of looking at something other than what is directly present, which we then (almost unconsciously) take hold of and avail ourselves of when making sense of what we think there is in the world around us. In this sense the rhetorical and allegorical text thus tells a story that fires the mind to a creative act through the (re)production of an idealised or poetic feeling that persuades or engages an interest which an author has identified beforehand. Accepting this expressionist reverie provides a dialectic theory that challenges the normal assumptions concerning recognition processes and proposes a two way possibility in the formation of understanding.

Commentary IV. Re-imaging the role of the imagination

Implicated in the above section is that the possibilities for generating emotional understanding calls for new conceptions of the possible relations and dependencies that exist between emotion and experience and that we need a more extensive theory of the mind than that common in conventional (realist and rationalist) ethnography in order to understand the politics of ethnographic conviction. Indeed we may need a post-structuralist idea of the mind, because what seems plausible in relation to the evocations of rhetorical and allegorical texts in the present consideration of them is that becoming aware is a process whereby *emotions evoke* certain *experiences* and *ideas* that they then also unite with, in one of (at least) two different ways. One is creative and experimental. The other is subject to ideological over-determination and hegemony, where (re)awakening stocks of knowledge (re-)produces the familiar worlds with which cultural members are in one sense already acquainted (Gubrium and Holstein,

1998). Together these two possibilities provide a situation where understanding will become caught up in practice in one of two kinds of articulation. One favours a radical renewal in understanding and the other favours the reproduction of dominant ideology.

The arousal of emotions and their association with ideas through a narrative in the (first) open, creative, un-restrained and experimental sense, is sometimes called the awakening of a metonymic understanding and is perhaps most relevant in literature, in writings like some of for instance Shakespeare's works (Derrida, 1994). Texts such as Hamlet's recollections to his servant (an example used by Derrida in recognition of Marx previous use) are good examples. Like a positive reading of Mulkay's moving story, these examples carry statements about the state of something not directly grasped but yet at least (spiritually) present and can open the imagination to new impulses. This concerns the issue of mediation, as is also taken up by Vygotsky (concerning cultural artefacts), by Marx in Brumaire and the thesis on Feuerbach (regarding history) and by Derrida (concerning the workings of civilisational ethos and its traces in everyday life in forms of understanding and forms of social representation: Derrida, 1976, 1991, 1994). However these ideas also give voice to a notion of a consciousness which is mediated by the imagination, a notion which comes I think initially from Aristoteles (although it was never finally developed by him) and then Kant (Helmstad, 1999), but which is also represented in the interpretative theories of Schleiermacher, Dilthey, Heidegger and Gadamer, who distinguish two uses of the imagination in understanding. One of these is in ordinary thought and perception. The other is in aesthetic experience (see also e.g. Palmer, 1969 and Helmstad, 1999). And when they are brought together when viewing an object that is present to the senses, experience embodies a 'synthesis' of two elements—one intuitive and the other conceptual, as also recognised by Bruner (1990, 1996) and Schwant (2000).

The above suggestions imply that mediation is important to understanding and that it includes the imagination as a constitutive part of the nature of the experience that expresses it. However, also stressed is that even this possibility is haunted by the revenant of past forms of representation. In the case of ethnographic writing this is a past that includes the hegemony of scientific writing in social science, where as culturally descriptive scientific writing, ethnographic texts have become trapped by a pursuit of (the myth of) an idealised objective relationship that disregards the (myth of the) subtlety of the subjective-concrete and particular (Lather, 2000; Tedlock, 2000) and suggests that ethnographic writing can only with some difficulty attain the reflexive qualities and form of literature, because to maintain its claims as science, it has to be concerned with things other than the interests and expressions of literature (which as opposed to science attend to diversity and the relationship between inner experience and social life). Ethnographic writing has to *converge* on something to be science, as science labels diversity and the relation of inner experience (emotion) to the socius as a source of error to be overcome rather than as a value to be celebrated, and has to in order to maintain its difference from (and advantage over) literature. And this is the strength of a rhetorical and allegorical text such as Mulkay's. He brings perception and aesthetic articulation together in an open reverie of form and content that closes on a convincing expressionist account of the history of science.

Bringing perception and aesthetic appreciation together in expressionistic writing provides an alternative form of representation in ethnography to the realist or impressionist forms of writing that seem to currently dominate it and sets the firing of the imagination up as perhaps the most crucial element of creative understanding by providing particular ideas about the relations between the intellectual content of the words of a story and the meanings and value which can be attributed to them. These words are synthesised into meaning content by an act of the imagination that constitutes them as an experience which the imagination then can either remain (temporarily) bound to or be creatively—playfully and experimentally—freed from (Derrida, 1976; Helmstad, 1999; Schwant, 2000).

This is a notion of the *semiotic mind* and has implications for ethnographic education/training concerning the generation of a critical awareness of textuality and writing practices, particularly with regard to how to make texts used and useful (see also Larsson, 1998; Clough, 2000). What it suggests is that we may need to develop our *playful*, emotional and (creatively) expressive capabilities as ethnographic writers, by *renewing* our epistemologies and developing an aesthetic capability, rather than simply honing our observational and reportorial skill, as it is in this way, I would suggest (i.e. by articulating the concept of semiotic mind in ethnography and by developing aesthetic capabilities), that we can live up to the promise of experimental writing, to critically engage with things which have political value and meaning (Clough, 2000). This also seems to be what Mulkay has accomplished when we critically consider the content, form and effects of his text.

What I am suggesting here is that when developing critical ethnographic skills (particularly of representation) we should draw attention more in the future than we have in the past to the creative process of using language in helping free alternative creations of meaning, by accepting that how we see the world depends both upon what is actually really materially present to and in it and our disposition to form beliefs about it. This is in its way also supported by Spivak (1993) who quotes Derrida when indicating that for its realisation, any thought requires *both* the principle of reason *and* the beyond of reason and that between the two, small differences can decide the outcome in the displaced passage of one term of opposition to another in our current economies of understanding. However the idea also has similarities with the development of identity as expressed in Grossberg (1996), with Bhaktin's valuations of the carnevalesque and with Helmstad's (1999) descriptions of 'the most advanced forms of understanding of understanding' (sic) and applies to how texts can be understood, both as texts and in terms of what the text describes (Marcus, 1998), to provide us with a notion of the *homo ludus* and a very different position to that of dominant psychology as to what constitutes the mind (as a rational entity) and understanding (as a rational practice). This difference applies I would suggest, not only to the versions of the mind and understanding in cognitivism, but even to the humanist views of mind in Dilthey's and Schleiermacher's hermeneutics and Husserlian transcendental phenomenology (Bleakley, 2000; Schwant, 2000).

Discussion

By the stories of the conventional (rationalist and realist, cognitivist and constructivist) *psychologies* of mind, it is suggested that objectively true knowledge is possible and that the imagination is an encumbrance to this. Further, that the mind can be freed from the imagination and all such concepts which oppose true knowledge, by becoming *free* to engage in the world *anew*, in a way that enables *genuine* concepts that bear objectively on a particular experience to develop (from Gadamar, 1993: 81-93; in Helmstad, 1999). This notion of the rational, purposive mind, gives a rationale for one of two distinct ways in which the content of experience is said to be provided. Both of these are relevant to ethnographic writing—although of course to different genres of it in different ways (and at different times: see also Atkinson, 1990; Hammersley, 1992; Viditch and Lyman, 1998; Marcus, 1998; Tedlock, 2000). The first relates to perception and communication in realist and impressionistic ethnography (also van Maanen, 1988). The second departs from ideas about the carnevalesque workings of a semiotic mind where ethnography is a primarily aesthetic and ethical experience and practice (Clough, 2000; Denzin, 2000; Lather, 2000; Tedlock, 2000). If the two are possible to bring together, my suggestion is that this could be in expressionistic writing where, as it were via an operative factor of a *playful* and reflexive linguistic turn, the writer tries to encourage *the play of the imagination as an inter-textual quality in the re-making of a sense of experience.*

Reference to the role of imagination as an inter-textual quality in the making of sense experience is also found in several other sources (e.g. Bengtsson, 1993; Bleakley, 2000; Schwant, 2000) and gives imagination a special value in the way in which a content and an experience become 'fused' as part of a creative capacity, or what Sartre refers to in the *Psychology of Imagination* (concerning imagining as 'the positing of an object as a nothingness' and as an *unbeing*) as a content that has no reality beyond our disposition to 'see' it. Such content is said to be that which is summoned by art when, for example, we see a face expressed in a picture of a forest or hear an emotion expressed in a piece of music (also Schwant, op cit.). However realistic the experience is felt to be, neither the face in the picture, the forest in the picture, nor the emotion in the notes played in the music are real, while both faces, forests and emotions are real in everyday life and experience. It is in this way that the senses of face, forest and emotion are real. They derive from an association with previous experiences in the firing of the imagination.

Encouraging (and helping) the firing of the imagination has some resemblance to some experiments across the common distinctions in semiotics between the sign and the signified and can form a space from which to forge a connection between the lived and the possible, as a faculty of mind and semiotic practice; something that has been put in a similar way (using different terminology) by Helmstad (1999) with regards to the play of the imagination with respect to the perceptual and grammatological elements of experience in the construction of understandings of understanding itself and that appeals also to the notion that thought and semiotic experiences are inseparable from the elements of the material culture of late-modernity that they relate to (see also Serematakis, 1994; Säljö, 2000; Alvesson and Deetz, 2000). This has important implications for ethnographic writing practices, as it questions whether doing and writing ethnography is nothing more (but also nothing less) than using the rules of a language game in what is principally a social and discursive practice in the processes of convincing others about (the values of) something you have come to deeply believe yourself. However, no matter how innocent, innocent or well-intentioned this 'aim to convince' may be, in terms of its art it likens deception as much as it does illumination (Tedlock, 2000). As Mulkay also puts it, perhaps this is finally always inevitably so:

> How can human language escape its essential character ... as a tool for controlling and refashioning the world? Is it not true that, in speaking, we project our speech outside itself, thereby creating the appearance of an independent world beyond our speech? Is it not true that we then have no option but to act as if the illusion created by our speech is the one real world in which we, and all others, have our and their being?
> (Mulkay, op cit., p 35-36)

This leaves us with yet another question. As Tedlock (op cit., p. 471) has expressed it, experience may be intersubjective, social, processual and embodied rather than absolute and fixed, and is therefore also dialogical, but given Mulkay's comments above, how can we devise textual structures that address us along with the content of our speech and which draw attention to the creative processes of using language toward an ever present possibility of alternative creations (Clough, 2000)? For isn't this possibility almost essential for ethnographic writing to be fair to those it portrays (Denzin, 2000).

Conclusions

Before the enlightenment, personal identities, knowledge and the social order (of things) were mediated through tradition(s) and dominating social narratives, as Alvesson and Deetz (2000) have pointed out. These were sometimes equally shared within a culture and sometimes enforced to the advantage of one group over another, through the exploitation of ignorance and the propagation of a fear of divine or other forms of retribution. After the enlightenment, in the West, the promise was an end to this kind of domination (which Kant called a self-imposed exile from personal freedom) through the development of an autonomic subject that gradually obtained enhanced degrees of liberty on the basis of a rational holding anticipated to develop from the ever increasing fold of scientific knowledge and scientific writing.

The enlightenment was in other words meant to mark the victory of rationalism over the darkness of an authority that had its basis solely in ideological domination, where all forms of power were based primarily on the enforced acceptance of traditional values. However, as critical theorists such as Adorno, Horkheimer, Habermas and Marcuse—and the various postmodernists such as Foucault, Derrida, Deleuze and Laclau—have pointed out, this *modernising* project of the enlightenment could never, and has never been able to attain such aims, as it too is built on an ambiguous authority, the mediation of mythical values and beliefs and (at times) the unnecessary use of force as well.

The present text makes suggestions about the writing and reading of ethnographic texts in what may be a post-structural movement, but it can still be accused of repeating the modernist narrative on the dilemma of difference and to have failed to open up to new forms of understanding, because it has finally remained within the strategic forms of modern logic (difference, individuality and temporality) that reproduce rather than contest the formations of modern power discourse. Mulkay suggests (op cit., p. 22) this problem is ultimately the problem of all disciplinary writing and cannot be escaped from, as such writing is always (by being of a discipline) also a part of a stratifying machine that reproduces the real as a relation of content and expression through the creation of subject-object abstractions and the positioning of subjectivity as value (Grossberg, 1996). On the basis of the archaeology of the present, this problem is suggested to be almost irredeemable in ethnography at the present time because although everyone exists within the strata of subjectivity, they are also located at particular positions, each of which enables and constrains the possibilities of experience, of representing those experiences and of legitimising those representations.

This returns us to the problem of the paralysing tautology of structuralist understandings of the world written on by Williams (1976) and echoed in Willis (1977). But it also leaves the opening question of the chapter about ethnographic representation as one of how access, investment, participation and the structure of belonging are distributed within ethnography's own particular domains. When ethnography is an epistemologically regional project (i.e. fully relativised) that uses and has always used what are basically (nothing more or less than) rhetorical tropes in the construction of its discourses, this positions ethnographic writing as less of a question of subjectivity than it is one of politics and intention, and means that when it comes to changing forms of ethnographic representation and ways of thinking about how and why the world presently appears to us as it does, this requires *both* the principle of reason *and* the agency beyond, where small differences can decide the outcome. The writing of ethnography is more of a political problem than it is an epistemological issue in this sense as changing forms of representation are not just the markings of a writing subject (an author), but also the constituting marks of an abode and an outcome of how empowerment is enabled at particular sites and along certain vectors in a way not reducible to epistemological positions of subjectivity alone (Beach, 1995; Grossberg, 1996).

Chapter 6

Artistic representation and research writing

Dennis Beach

Introduction

This chapter has been written mainly on the basis of an article published previously in the international research journal *Refelctive Practice* (Carfax) which was about the effects of the literary turn in social science and the crisis of representation on the practice of professional research writing, which became 'seen as' and 'represented as' more rhetorical than realist as objective truth quests became considered as impossible projects. This opened the way for a plethora of experimental forms of writing in ethnography as alternatives to conventional scientific realism in our writing (van Maanen, 1988; Richardson, 1992; Viditch and Lyman, 1994; Denzin and Lincoln, 1994; Clough, 2000; Ellis, 2000; Geertz, 1983). In the sense of Gubrium and Holstein (1997: 92), it is my hope that by reflexively examining (these) representational practices, something helpful might be said about how meaning can be constituted in research writing in its *new* experimental moment.

A double realisation is important if critical possibilities are to be kept alive within the relativistic moment. The first part of this double realisation involves grasping that we (as writers) operate under conditions of uncertainty and indeterminacy and the second part is about still finding ways to write critically and meaningfully towards a politics of the future with this in mind. Without arguing against her positioning of reflexive social science research writing as somewhere in the margins between claims of truth and claims of textuality, I am in a sense arguing both for and against Britzman's (1995) assertions that such writing is not able to reliably inform institutional policy, practices and professions.

The styles and techniques of *bricolage* and collage

Denzin and Lincoln (1994) argue that research work in ethnography and other forms of qualitative research, is at least in one sense *bricolage*, in that such forms are at one and the same time *both* a construction made from the artefacts found in a particular situation *and* the technique or way of putting these together for communication purposes (also Scheurich, 1997). This view fits in with the term *bricolage* in art as the use of *ready-mades* or 'whatever comes to hand' in the construction of a tableau. Scheurich (1997: 55) expresses *bricolage* as follows: *Bricolage* is a French word which means the *ad hoc* assemblage of miscellaneous materials and signifying structures (Levi-Strauss, quoted in Norris, 1987, p. 134). Spivak (1976) says the *bricoleur* makes do with things that were meant perhaps for other ends (p. xix). (But) Levi-Strauss used this word to describe how pre-Western cultures made sense of the World in a way quite remote from our own, more logical and regimented habits of thought (Norris, 1987, 134). The *bricoleur* is a kind of Heath Robinson figure, happy to exploit the most diverse assortment of mythemes—or random combinatory elements—in order to create a working hypothesis about this or that feature of social life. The opposite approach is that of the typecaste engineer, one who sets out with a well defined concept of a machine (or explanatory theory) he wants to construct, and who follows this blueprint through to its logical conclusion.

Of course Levy Strauss may have been wrong about 'The Savage Mind' and Norris may have exaggerated his distinctions, but when we think about it, equating the representation of culture with (or as) *Bricolage* as a primitive (pre-modern) *and ad hoc activity* as opposed to a form of type-caste engineering (such as structural equation modelling perhaps), re-asserts a time typical late-modern binary between anti positivist and logical-positivist approaches to research that is often romantically embraced in ethnography as appropriate for describing the move to qualitative research work. But the question is, in what way is *bricolage* really a suitable metaphor for ethnography? Are we not being over-romantic when ethnographic writing forms are equated with *bricolage*?

In answer to this I would say that ethnographic writing is not *bricolage* and that the terms collage and collage making provide more promising metaphors because whilst bricoleurship may be an adequate metaphor for certain aspects of assembly in data-organisation and pre-analytic work, it is not adequate towards the final, written, ethnographic research report or thesis as these 'structures' combine textual elements that are far more *refined* than *ready-mades* and that have been crafted together with particular points or sets of points in mind (also van Maanen, 1988; Sanjek, 1990; Clifford, 1990; Atkinson, 1990; Beach, 2002).

Collage is originally a French term meaning pasting and is an artistic technique of applying manufactured, printed, or found materials, such as bits of newspaper, fabric, wallpaper, etc., to a panel or canvas in combination with painting, to produce an image which expresses some kind of feeling. This implies that *bricolage* and collage are not the same thing, and that the sophistication and intentions behind the production of research texts would also place them closer to collage than to *bricolage*. This is also the point of ethnography. Ethnographers actually produce rather than collect the data from which they 'fashion', their accounts in ways that involve rather more than merely making do with in some *ad hoc* way piecing together whatever might be available (see also e.g. Tyler, 1987; van Maanen, 1988; Clifford, 1990; Sanjek, 1990; Atkinson, 1990; Beach, 1995, 2002; Arnstberg, 1997; Dreissen, 1993). Collage is *composed*. It consists of things like old engravings and prints that have been deliberately cut and pasted together in order to convey some kind of message or feeling with a refinement that makes *bricolage* seem amateurish and open-ended by comparison. There is a message intended here. This concerns *the crafting of a text* rather than merely making do with sticking bits of raw data together in the belief that these will speak for themselves. As Geetz, 1983, 1988) suggests (see also Atkinson, 1990 and Willis, 2000) ethnography is a craft of artful composition.

Visual montage

Visual montage works through juxtaposing images to produce an impression or to illustrate an association of ideas which press beyond surface representations and is carried out when composite photographic images are made either by pasting together individual prints or parts of prints, or by successively exposing individual images onto a single paper simultaneously through superimposed negatives to break with the normal realist conventions of natural history and or chronological sequencing, such as in the film *Strike* (1924), where the Russian director Sergey Eisenstein juxtaposes scenes of people being cut down during a workers strike with a shot of cattle being slaughtered. Montage is in this sense, like in a way collage is, an editing technique for assembling separate pieces of film into a sequence to supply a particular message, to reinforce a point or to enhance a story telling capacity. And it is in this sense that it has relevance to representations in ethnographic writing.

Montage is not new in ethnography. Indeed it has been documented since the pioneering days of ethnographic fieldwork in the sequencing of subtexts in narrative writing and life-history research. With montage, portions of pictures (or texts) can be carefully built up piece by piece by cutting and fitting each part with the others to make a story which is actually (then) put together from separate sources made at separate space-time locations, but which are 'clipped together' thematically in a manner which also provides an effect of some kind of continuity. We might think of films such as Tarrantino's *Pulp Fiction* or *Kill Bill* in this sense in a film medium. Where as collage may use textuality, imagery and material textures at the same time (in the same picture) to address an idea, montage concentrates more on one (or two) media at a time (sequentially) in the creation of a story.

Prosaic iconography: Pop-art and ethnography

Prosaic iconography is a style of expression which is distinguished by its degrees of irregularity, variety and close approximation to the patterns of communication in everyday life and an art of representation by means of matching images (also Atkinson, 1990). Prosaic iconography is particularly common as a form of representation in Pop-art, a largely British and American movement which was given its name because of its portrayal of any and all aspects of popular culture in contemporary life with images that were generally taken from the mix of contemporary popular media (television, comic books, movie magazines and forms of advertising). The term was of course also a generally taken and accepted one for music forms of the same era, which shared a similarly acknowledged prosaic character.

In ethnography an approach likening Pop-art has been possible to recognise since the pioneering days of 'anthropological sociology' in the work of Robert Parke and Robert Redfield in the Chicago School of Sociology who were both supporters of the use of any contemporarily available materials in research representations and who regularly used newspaper cut-outs, common pictures and textual thematisations of contemporary film media in their work (see also Junker, 1960; Blumer, 1969; van Maanen, 1988; Beach, 2003). These materials formed what were then (and still are) termed soap, although the term in common use often refers to the representation of daily life-like scenarios in contemporary TV-media for entertainment purposes.

This strategy of using 'soap' has been passed down through generations of subsequent Chicago scholars and their followers, including Herbert Blumer, Raymond Gold, Howard Becker and Erving Goffman, who all drew on whatever sources and materials became available to them (including those of contemporary media) in order to caste light on the issues their research became most concerned with and although no-one thought of calling these works *Pop-art scientific fictions*, maybe they could have, as this would seem to be particularly appropriate term for work such as that by Spradley and Mann (the cocktail waitress), Goffman's representations of institutions (as in e.g. *Asylums*), Leibow's *Tally's Corner* and

Whyte's *Street-corner Society*. All these authors have connections to the Chicago School or have been influenced by it and all their texts used aspects of romantic fiction in the construction of style and in order to exploit popular cultural images in the exploration of what were contemporary social scenes and situations.

The popularity of Pop-art in the 1960s and 1970s is often said to be because of its close reflection of the contemporary social situation of those whose life it also described. It was described as a down to earth art-form that ironised with the highbrow tendencies in previous art forms, by art-critics who revered it. However, this view can be challenged. The popularity of pop-art could equally well have been because its images were just aesthetically pleasing through their vivid contrasts of colour and form, a notion that is also supported by the idea that whilst Pop-art was initially a nihilistic kind of movement that ridiculed the seriousness of other art and tried to narrow the distance between art and life by celebrating mass-produced objects and the commercial materials of the machine-age (like beer cans and other similar objects, see for instance Warhol's *Campbel's Soup Can* and *Volkswagon* Beetle), like music by the cult-band The Doors, it finally fell prey to commercial strategists who exploited it heavily in marketing and advertising.

Maybe the use of contemporary figures by ethnographers can seem to suffer the same demise. Willis textual (re)creation and use of *the Lads* to illustrate aspects of male-working-class style, Patrick's similar details of Glasgow street-gang youth, Whyte's descriptions of Doc and Cornerville and Leibow's of Tally Jackson, all exploit easily recognised elements of popular culture in portrayals of school and contemporary street life and are all also representations of profane culture which can be re-appropriated by capital in various ways. This kind of problem has been discussed by Willis (1999: 158) as follows:

> (T)he capitalist cultural commodity circuit keeps on dipping back into the streets and trawling the living culture for ideas for its next commodity, its next circuit. Capital's cultural producers remorselessly ransack the everyday in their never ending search to find, embody and maximise all possible use values in products. The usefulness of the new or more developed communicative forms produced and shared in real informal communities of meaning is precisely the quality that attracts the predators, even as they deny it by plunging into further commodity relations (in an) attempt to realise the value of informal production in the traditional capitalist form of money.

What is being implied above is that the simplicity, accessibility and readily assimilated nature of Pop art is quite compelling perhaps to ethnographic writers, who are seeking to both make accessible and at times 'popularise' their texts, but that on reflection this also has its down side in something which even became visible in later developments in Pop art itself. From a starting point in ironicising examples of media imagery, the accessibility of Pop art representations and their ready comprehension helped to render it exploitable by exactly those groups whose very life-style and values it had initially mocked and it was colonised and taken over by the mass media itself as its own form of popular imagery. In this way the art that had initially claimed to show us an alienated life form was now being used as a representation of commodity advertising itself.

Realism

The conception of philosophical realism is that the objects of sensory perception or of cognition are real in their own right and exist independently of the mind. This is also recognised in representations in artistic realism where the aim is to capture and portray something which is felt to genuinely exist in itself by *capturing and showing* the universals, principles and rules that realists believe govern the classification of things in everyday life. Such a classification occurs when for instance one classifies an ambiguous wooden object as a rice-flail for instance, instead of as a weapon, even when the nature of the correctness of the classification itself is questionable. Realists assert that classification reflects distinctions inherent in the world, which puts them in a position of contrast to idealists and conceptualists who only see universal reality as a mental concept— and nominalists who restrict reality even further to mere names.

Realism holds that the senses afford knowledge of the distinct, real existence of independent objects in space and time and realist writing in ethnography attaches onto this idea, in that it is claimed that realist researchers tap into something already present (whether this be a materially real or an assumed really existing mental or social representation) which they then describe with a neutral and objective language. Realism in this sense attaches objective qualities to things that are also said to exist independently of our engagements with them in representational practices. However, the difficulty for the realist is that the experiences on the basis of which one knows about such objects are always themselves finally private and depend on the mind for their existence and nature as the realist seeks a link that permits knowledge of one kind of thing on the basis of another without resorting to solipsism. Opponents of course charge that this leads inevitably to solipsism in any account of inter-subjective action.

Realist writing tended to dominate the Golden Ages of qualitative research and ethnographic writing (see Denzin and Lincoln, 1994; Viditch and Lyman, 1994; Van Maanen, 1988), even though it has now given way to the impressionistic and the confessional tales of the field, both of which represent a revolt against realist traditions, although quite different ones. The realist position has become increasingly difficult since the so called literary turn in the social sciences, even though in some moderate form researchers can and do often still try to write realist texts. Perhaps this is to some degree inevitable. For as Mulkay has put it:

> ... can human language escape its essential character... as a tool for controlling and refashioning the world? Is it not true that, in speaking, we project our speech outside itself, thereby creating the appearance of an independent world beyond our speech? Is it not true that we then have no option but to act as if the illusion created by our speech is the one real world in which we, and all others, have our and their being? (How can we) devise textual structures which address us along with the content of our speech and which draw attention to the creative processes of using language and, thereby to the ever present possibility of alternative creations?   (Mulkay, op cit., pp. 35-36)

Some writer-critics of realism (e.g. Richardson, 1994; Lather and Smithies, 1997; Clough, 2000) see realist narrative as a power-text which inevitably tends towards totalistic claims and treacherous translation (see also Lather, 1991; Britzman, 1995). When conveying (or attempting to convey) elements in the world, writing impressionistically is felt by these authors to be both more tenable and more honest, as it is felt to be more genuinely representational to the impressions of the real on the senses or the authors vision/view. In contrast to realist writing, impressionistic writing is said to lift out textures of possible meaning rather than claiming to show an absolute truth in a single form. This way of research writing has almost become favoured practice in ethnography since the rhetorical/literary turn in anthropology and the social sciences (also van Maanen, 1988; Beach, 2002).

Impressionism

Impressionist painting developed chiefly in France during the late 19th and early 20th centuries and chiefly comprises the work of artists who shared a set of related approaches and techniques, the most conspicuous of which was an attempt to *record an experience* of visual reality in terms of transient effects of light and colour or, in other words, to convey visual impressions (cf. Ash, 1988). This was not done through the conventions of realist painting and its tones of brown and green however (as in conventional landscape paintings and portraits), but through the use of exaggerated brush-strokes and a mixture of vivid and contrastive colour combinations to emphasise the play of light and shade on the senses. In ethnographic writing this contrasting of colours by the artist is called brash juxtaposition, a brash comparison which can enliven the imagination as to the possible texture of the object of representation itself (see e.g. Geertz critically revered text on the Balineese cock fight: Geertz, 1973).

The impressionist painters shared a common dissatisfaction with the conventional treatments of academic painting and sought a new aesthetic standard in which the importance of the traditional subject matter was downgraded and attention was shifted to the artist's manipulation of colour, tone and texture as ends in themselves in such a way that the subject of the painting became a vehicle for the artful composition of areas of flat colour, where perspective depth was minimised and a primacy placed instead on surface patterns (also Ash, 1988). This focuses the surface relationships in the picture rather than the illusory three-dimensional space which the picture creates in realism.

To help their art, impressionists adopted a practice of painting entirely out-of-doors while looking at the actual scene, instead of finishing up a painting from sketches in the studio. This also fits with what the impressionists are said to have been setting out to reproduce in their work, this being the manifold effects of direct and reflected light, which they sought to build up out of discrete flecks and dabs of colour that were intended to evoke the variations of hue produced by sunlight and its reflections (Ash, 1988). In this way forms lose their clear outlines and become shimmering and vibrating re-creations of actual outdoor conditions. The similarities of this within ethnography lie particularly with the *situation* of journal, diary and field-note writing during ethnographic fieldwork (Sanjek, 1990; Clifford, 1990; Beach, 1997, 2002). These texts are actually *made* from impressions created by the play of elements of culture, in an ethnographic involvement with it.

According to Beach (2001) Impressionist painting embraced a certain sense of relief for the artists pursuing it from their experienced restrictions of the conventions of former artistic styles and provided an impetus which freed all Post-Impressionist artists such as Cézanne, Degas, Gauguin, the younger van Gogh, and Seurat from traditional techniques and approaches to subject matter in a manner paralleling van Maanen's description of 'impressionist tales of the field', where the literary or even poetic effect is primary and is intended to allow an author to exaggerate in order to make a point. Kvale (1996) claims that impressionist accounts can represent things more effectively than realist ones, provided the narrative ingenuity of the writer is effectively brought forward (also Larsson, 1998, 2000). This puts emphasis on the literary (writing and authorship) skills of the researcher and her/his knowledge of audience (Beach, 2002).

Expressionism

Emotion and other strong feelings are often denied space in scientific experiences and scientific writing, however many forms of qualitative research such as auto-Ethnography, Life History and Narrative research deal with and are unavoidably coloured by emotional experiences and closeness in the field, and empathy and subjectivity are considered to be fundamental to a research account, in a situation where the researcher, her senses and charged sensibilities form the key instrument of the research. This puts the researcher's emotions, subjectivity and empathy right in the centre of research work. But these are dealt with in different ways in different traditions. For instance in realist work according to Beach (2001) the emotions and emotionally laden data are controlled for, marginalised and even limited if possible, as they are seen as sources of potential error and bias in the objective account of the research (also Hammersley, 2002), whilst in other genres the value of emotion and feeling are recognised and given space in communication about real pressures and presence in the field. This is particularly the case in expressionist forms of research communication.

In art, expressionism developed as a tradition and a style of representation which was felt to be most suitable for getting (and was perhaps even intended to get) the charged *emotion* of an experience into a communicative media. This was because in expressionism, rather than seeking to depict an objective reality, the artist sought to voice to the subjective emotions and responses that objects and events aroused in her/him. This was often done through a distortion, exaggeration, primitivism and fantasy which aimed to produce a vivid, jarring, violent, or dynamic effect with an exaggeration or primitivism going back to the roots of the German Expressionist school, as well as the works of van Gogh, Munch, and Ensor, each of whom used the expressive possibilities of colour and line to explore dramatic and emotion-laden themes in order to help convey qualities of fear, horror, and the grotesque or celebrate nature with hallucinatory intensity (Beach, 2001). In this way these artists broke away from the literal representation of realist nature, as did impressionists too of course, but this time in order to express more subjective outlooks or a state of mind.

The distinctions between impressionist and expressionist breaks with realism are both political and profound in my view, and are central aspects for consideration in the development of representation in ethnography for these reasons. The impressionist break was about freeing the artist from the prison of convention so s/he could explore an expanded terrain of personal freedom for creativity. The expressionist break was about using whatever tools art gave to enable the artist to express her/his anguish about the current state of things in the world.

The distinctions between impressionism and expressionism in the above senses are perhaps clearest with respect to a second and principal wave of Expressionism, which began about 1905, when a group of German artists led by Kirchner formed a loose association called Die Brücke. This group included Heckel, Schmidt-Rottluff, and Bleyl (Konstlexion, op cit)—all painters who were in revolt against what they saw *as the superficial naturalism of a decadent academic Impressionism* and who wanted to re-infuse art with a vigour they felt it lacked, and they sought to do this through an elemental, primitive, highly personal and spontaneous expression, which developed a style notable for its harshness, boldness, and intensity. They used jagged and distorted lines as well crude and rapid brushwork with jarring colours, to depict urban street scenes and other contemporary subjects in an emotionally charged manner. And in this sense it is often felt that their works express frustration, anxiety, disgust, discontent and violence in a frenetic intensity of feeling, in response to the ugliness and the crude banality which they felt were the central features and contradictions of modern life. Expressionist painting thus seemed to suit an atmosphere of cynicism, alienation, and disillusionment as *a reaction against materialism, complacent bourgeois prosperity, rapid mechanisation and urbanisation.*

The expressionist movement became the dominant movement in Germany during and immediately after World War I. This was close in time to the growth of the Frankfurt School of social theory (also Held, 1980) and like the Frankfurt School, many expressionist painters and dramatists were also hounded by the National Socialists and the movement itself was outlawed by Hitler in the inter-war years, creating a similarity between expressionist and neo-Marxist writing. But on reflection, such similarities exist at several levels. For instance, the aim of expressionist play-writers and novelists is often said to have been to forge a drama of social protest which aimed to convey their concern with the horrific general truths embedded in particular social situations and sets of relations. Specific instances here served as illustrative of these general truths or principles. This is also a leading theme in critical social science (also Fay, 1977) and critical ethnography (Beach, 1997, 2001, 2002, 2003; Carspecken, 1995; Willis, 2000). In Willis terms (1977: from Beach, 1995, p. 23) this is an aim to show in graphic detail the cultural viewpoint of the oppressed, the 'hidden' knowledge and resistance as well as the basis on which entrapping decisions are taken in some sense of liberty, but which nevertheless help to produce 'structure'.

The concern for showing general truths through specific empirical instances was expressed as essential in the deconstruction of ideological domination and material exploitation under capitalism by Marx and Engels (see e.g. the final chapter in Capital, vol. 3) and is to be found in neo-Marxist ethnographic work and the vivid writing of the Centre for Contemporary Cultural Studies (CCCS) group at Birmingham University (often called the Birmingham School and whose own writing can therefore be used as illustrative, together also with work by the cultural theorist Raymond Williams (see also Kuper, 1987). In the same sense that expressionist writers explored the predicaments of representative symbolic types rather than of fully developed individualised characters in their plays, so too has the CCCS explored symbolic tropes in their works, which all attend in some way or another to the drama of general life and the reproduction of alienated life-forms.

Similar styles of writing to expressionist drama are found in life-history and critical narrative research writing, in which; as in expressionist drama; the leading character of the life-history or narrative work is able to pour out her/his woes in long monologues which are couched in a concentrated, elliptical, almost tele-grammatic language (see also Shakespeare's *Hamlet* in this respect). The immediate task at hand of these monologues can vary. They may for instance set out to explore something like the spiritual malaise of youth, its revolt against an older generation or dominant order, or the various political or revolutionary remedies that have presented themselves to the writer (e.g. Willis, op cit.; Mac an Ghail, 1988; Hall and Jefferson, 1978). Opposition, resistance or revolt against injustice, oppression or marginalisation are the common mythemes explored here. As in Orwell's works, malaise, frustration and alienation are other common themes (Beach, 2001, 2002).

Expressionist poetry is a derivative literary genre of the expressionist movement which in ethnography is perhaps most closely approximated by metonymic texts like that of Mulkay's moving story of love and bondage in Mulkay (1989; Beach, 2002), Laurel Richardsons (1992) life of an unwed mother (Louisa May) or my own story of the destruction of early childhood teacher education curriculum possibilities and progressivist student professional identity development in *The Child and the Struggle* (Beach, 2005). Like expressionist drama, expressionist poetry refers essentially to individual detail primarily as illustration, and appears to seek an ecstatic lyricism by using strings of nouns, few adjectives and infinitive verbs, eliminated narrative and description to get at the essence of feeling, which are all accessible techniques for ethnographers of course. However, even more compelling in expressionist poetry is the strength of similarity between this genre in general and sub-themes around the evolution of a sense of horror and an apocalyptic vision of the collapse of civilisation, within which traditional bourgeois values (such as charity and consensus institutions) can be satirised whilst values which are more concerned with political and social reform and which express the hope for a coming revolution can be revered and admired.

Conclusion

Writing in 1996, The Danish educational anthropologist-ethnographer Karin Borgnakke referred to four cardinal points of ethnographic work. These apply also to other forms of critical research in the social sciences (Alvesson and Deetz, 2000). The first concerns the choice of topic of the research and its justification. The second concerns moving from choice of topic through a delimitation of the problem area to the formulation of the problem. The third concerns defining the area to be investigated, carrying out the investigation and writing it up. And the fourth means moving from the continuous process of internal assessment to an external evaluation of the critical and political implications of the work (see also Denzin, 2000 and Clough, 2000). These four cardinal points chart the course of an ethnographic research project according to Borgnakke.

The present paper has been very much concerned with the processes of representation and the organisational frames for *writing out about* a research project in a research thesis, paper or report. It began by in a sense questioning a naive empiricist trope (*bricolage*). It hopefully then went on to present alternative organisational frames. However as Kvale (1996) also indicates, the purpose of highlighting such different forms for organising writing is not to privilege one (e.g. realist fiction, the expressionist poem, textual montage) above the others, or to designate the one true form for reporting and writing ethnographically under all conditions. Indeed I think the post-foundational and post-structural turns in the social and literary sciences and philosophy have set a stop for this, so the intention is more to try to provide a discourse concerning the availability and characteristics of different writing styles, their injunctions with critical or other intentions and the ways they can be drawn together in a reflexive writing project. The hope is, that by being more aware of how what we write can be formed to some specific ends of communication, we can balance a written text in a way that opens new possibilities for getting ideas across. Perhaps, as put by Ellis (2000), the suggestion is that we might try to engage *both* sides of the brain at once, by encouraging a semiotic reflexivity *and* a primary mediation of the body memory to interplay back and forth, *until thinking and feeling merge* (Ellis, 2000, p 273; also Helmstad, 1999). This relates to a notion of understanding beyond that of the semiotic mind and an aim to provoke a vexed agency in a quest re-wrest control from a post-modern, post-structuralist representational crisis over what to do in critical research writing (Clough, 2000). My hope is that by giving voice to and helping bring to a level of conscious awareness much of that which can be simply accepted as tacit knowledge in writing practices in ethnography more telling, feeling, practically *meaningful* texts might be written.

First there is a hoped for connection in reading the article itself, which it is hoped will engage a form of *self-reflection* or *introspection*, as a reflective examination of one's beliefs or motives as a writer. However, reflection is a term with several practical meanings. These include reflection as the *return of* something, such as light or sound waves from a particular surface (as in the production of a mirror image); the meaning of reflection as an abstraction or *transformation* of a figure in mathematics, in which each of the points in a figure are symmetrically *shifted* with respect to a defined line or plane; reflection as an action of bending or *folding back*; reflection as an effect produced by an *influence* (as in e.g. the high crime rate is a reflection of society); or reflection as something which is meant in the sense of a *reproach*, as in an indirect criticism, such as *her/his bad behaviour is a reflection on her/his bad character*. A reflection can also be a *thought*, an idea, an opinion formed, or a remark made as a result of a particular event; e.g. *my reflections on this situation are ...* .

All the above meanings comply with the etymology of the term reflection and all have a place in the present chapter. Their differences concern in a sense the subject matter of the chapter and its purpose. For instance, taking the crime-rate example, the subject is criminal behaviour, the idea is more specifically the causes of criminal behaviour, and the purpose is (it seems to me) to reproach current social orders and to indicate a possibility of a brighter or better future if certain changes to could be made to this order. This is really the sense in which reflection is hoped to become most engaged in the chapter with regard to writing as a reflective practice that can be improved by thoughtful consideration about how what we write can be formed as critical communication (see also Clough, 2000). This is perhaps clearest through my own sympathies for the expressionist form within a post-colonial politics of representation.

Emphasising a post-colonial aspect here accords with both Clough (op cit.), Mulkay (op cit.) and Moore and Bruder (1996, p. 636), who have all in their way remarked on how, although modern culture has standardised the scientific method and its forms of direct referencing in the conventional scientific realist tale (also van Maanen, 1988) as the preferred way to represent knowledge for comparison and validation processes even (until recently) in ethnography (also Atkinson, 1990), other cultures have other agreements and traditions and not to consider these alternative forms of representation risks missing an important philosophical point. This is that any way of knowing and its forms of representation are intimately bound up with meta-physical understandings about the nature of the world and existence(s) in it, so that a challenge to representational forms is also a challenge to claims about the truth, and more importantly in some senses, a potential challenge to the deepest beliefs within a civilisation, culture or group. This is a point of no small significance for post-colonial thought, which deals in part with the effects of precisely such challenges. Perhaps the chapter might therefore finally reflect a contribution to critical, post-structural, post-colonial writing in ethnography as a critically reflective practice in the transformational sense of the term reflect. That is at least my hope.

Chapter 7

Tales from the interface:
Disseminating ethnography for policy making

Geoff Troman

Introduction

The nature of the relationship between research and practice in any particular case is a negotiated one, in which the interests and power of others may play as significant a role as the views of researchers. This means that in the design of any inquiry researchers have to take account of what is feasible in the circumstances, as well as of more abstract arguments about the proper role of research. There are situations in which researchers can produce information which will directly serve the needs of policy makers or practitioners. However, very often these needs are not well defined, and/or are not a matter of consensus, nor will they necessarily remain the same over the course of the research. Moreover while the researcher's main concern may be to produce a valid account of the situation, very often policy makers and practitioners will be at least concerned with the implications of the findings in the context of current internal and external relations. How researchers position themselves in relation to these needs and concerns, and changes in them, will depend partly on the nature of their research goals, but also on the character of any initial research contract and on what sort of resolution to any conflict it is possible to negotiate. In this sense, even if in not other, research is a political enterprise.

(Hammersley, 1996)

Researchers now often enter collaborative relationships with and for powerless and marginalised groups, and through such relationships provide them with a vehicle for voicing their concerns and aspirations.

(Raymond Lee, 1993)

Introduction

At the time of the research reported in this chapter, educational research was in turmoil following recent largely negative official reviews of its practices and products (Bassey, 1998). It was held to be often of poor quality and biased (Ofsted/Tooley, 1998), did not involve 'users' (policy makers and practitioners) and was often remote from their needs and inaccessible to them (DfEE/Hillage et al. 1998). Although these latter critics acknowledged the difficulties involved in training 'users' to access research, and pointed out that successive governments had not used research findings in policy formation when they were available, they laid considerable responsibility for the current 'awful reputation' (Sroufe, 1997) of educational research firmly on educational researchers. The redemption of research was seen by these writers to involve a shake up of the organisation, funding and practices of the social research establishment, thereby introducing rigour and relevance. And also in the development of evidence-based practice and policy (Hargreaves, 1996) with some advocating the establishment of a 'science of teaching' (Reynolds, 1998).

These reviews fail to acknowledge that the policies of major research funding bodies had in fact been shaping the nature of research they were willing to fund. The Economic and Social Research Council (ESRC), for example, is a funding body which:

> ... has also been affected by the transformation of the public sector and has been pressured to adopt 'relevance' as an important criteria (sic) for funded research (ESRC, 1987). It now encourages far more applied research than in the past, requires evidence of utility to users, promotes greater academic-industry linkages and has strengthened the measures of accountability for those who receive money.   (Tritter, 1995, p.421)

The strong critiques of educational research ignore two decades of debate within the sociology of education, and other social science disciplines, on the relationship between research and policy/practice (Hammersley, 1994; Woods and Pollard, 1988; Finch, 1985; Rist, 1984; Pollard, 1984). The official reviewers also eschew a considerable body of literature which examines, in the context of educational research, the problematics of the theory/practice relationship (see for example, Hammersley, 1992; Hirst, 1983; Carr, 1987; Stenhouse, 1975; Kemmis, 1988; Gitlin, et al. 1993).

Since the 1960s in the United Kingdom qualitative methods have grown in importance within educational research, filling the 'void left by the demise' of quantitative approaches (Rist, 1984, p.159). However, qualitative studies are claimed to have had little impact on education policy (Hammersley, 1994; Halpin and Troyna, 1994). Despite reservations about reliability and generalisability in interpretative sociological approaches they were thought comparable to quantitative studies (previously attractive to policy makers) in terms of validity (Pollard, 1984) and could develop micro and macro theory and could and should inform policy and practice (Pollard, 1984; Finch, 1985; Woods and Pollard, 1988). Indeed, Rist (1984) argues that qualitative researchers are well placed to provide the type of knowledge needed by policy makers. Ethnographers, for instance, 'analyse in an ecologically valid manner the values, beliefs, settings and interactions of the participants'. And 'they can go backstage to participate in events that never meet the public eye so the participants' behaviours and beliefs are examined in context' (ibid. p. 160 and p. 163). This 'grounded' approach enables ethnographers to 'speak with authority, with a sense of how things really are' (ibid. p. 165). Thus the ethnographic method can yield rich data which has the capacity to show the impact of social policies on participants; this knowledge can subsequently inform policy change. Additionally, that ethnographic enquiry should be carried out in collaboration with 'users' has long been an argument made by leading researchers in this field for some time (see for example Woods and Pollard, 1988).

This chapter focuses on my involvement in an ethnographic research project directed by Peter Woods and funded by the ESRC. The title of the project was 'The Social Construction of Teacher Stress'. The research, which was planned and commenced prior to the official reports referred to previously, was judged to be relevant to teachers, other professions and policy makers. It involved collaboration between the researcher and 'users' at all stages of the project and a central aim was to inform policy at national, local and school level by the use of a variety of dissemination strategies. The chapter, while giving details of the whole project, concentrates on one aspect which was unanticipated at the outset of the project; a case study of a teacher self-help group. This development required a shift toward critical ethnographic methodology. It is argued that the issues raised by the researcher's involvement with participants in this case study have implications for critical ethnography in policy-related research.

Before discussing the study it is necessary to provide essential details of the research aims, approach and methods used in data collection and analysis.

The stress research: aims and processes

We thought the research topic to be of particular relevance to practitioners and policy makers as estimated numbers of teachers experiencing stress related illness and those retiring early on grounds of ill health were rising sharply (Woods, 1985; Troman, 2000; ; Troman and Woods, 2001; Brown and Ralph, 1998). Psychological studies (Travers and Cooper, 1996) confirmed that stress did seem to be a particular problem in the teaching profession. International research (reported in Vandenberghe and Huberman, 1999) suggested that teacher stress was not restricted to the United Kingdom and was not only an important issue for educational researchers, because:

> ... as an empirical phenomenon, it also has more immediate, practical consequences. ... (There) are multiple studies showing that burnout affects the quality of teachers' professional performance, their level of commitment, and their job satisfaction. It also appears to affect pupils' learning negatively and places a heavy burden on the school as workplace—for example, in collegial relations, in the quality of school climate. Even from a financial and economic point of view, there are consequences in terms of increased costs.
> (Kelchtermans and Strittmatter, 1999, p. 304)

The research was also relevant to researchers working in sociology of education for it was engaging with the 'core sociological issues of the relationship of the individual to society, of agency and constraint, control and order' (Pollard, 1992, p. 119). While Woods (1996a, p. 1) argued that stress was a:

> ... multi-dimensional and multi-levelled phenomenon, and personal (micro) situational (meso) and structural factors are involved in its production. It is an individually experienced phenomenon which is socially produced. There are certainly the personal elements of personality, commitment, career and role, and values involved. There are situational ones, too, of school organisation, teacher culture and teacher/pupil relationships. However, there are also wider factors such as the wholesale restructuring of schools and teaching which has been taking place in recent years.

The multi-dimensional stress research which was called for here seeks interrelationships and forms links with the micro, meso and macro rather than treating them as discrete levels (Kelchtermans, 1995). As A. Hargreaves (1998, p. 422) argues, these levels are not 'tightly insulated from one another' and 'structure and agency are relationally connected'. In work on the social construction of teacher stress we must avoid analyses which 'force a false separation of self, structure and situation into different sites of experience' (ibid.). What is really important, Hargreaves argues, is that we seek to understand how 'structures exert their effects and with what consequences and implications for the self, in different places and times' (ibid.).

The stress research sought to develop a number of theoretical areas. These were summarised in the proposal as follows:

(a) Intensification of work;

(b) Stress and burnout;

(c) Coping strategies;

(d) Dilemmas, tensions and constraints;

(e) Status passage;

(f) Teacher self, role and career.

The aims and objectives of the research were strongly policy related and were summarised in the proposal as:

(1) To explore the interconnections between micro, meso and macro factors in the production and experience of teacher stress. In particular, within that relationship, to consider:

♦   the part played by the changing nature of work;

♦   the part played by gender and role;

(2) To consider the effects of teacher stress on teacher self and identity; and on teaching and learning;

(3) To consider the factors leading to self-renewal and recovery from stress;

(5) To inform policy and practice relating to teacher stress at all three levels of macro (government policy), meso (school policy), and micro (teacher practice); and to seek ways in which the research may relate to, and inform, other professions; including using insights generated by the research to inform practitioners' (occupational health professionals) inservice training activities with school personnel and other professional groups; also to assist teachers in their own professional reflection on their experiences;

(6) To develop research methods appropriate to the research, including

collaborative research methods with teachers and with occupational health professionals.

Most research on teacher stress has adopted large-scale survey methods (for example, Travers and Cooper, 1996). By way of contrast, our stress research was qualitative in nature. The approach was ethnographic for I agree with Seddon (1998, p. 1) when she argues that:

> Ethnography is a key research strategy in such historic times of change. It provides a window into the practical realities of people's work and lives. It shows the constraints and contradictions that they face and reveals the way they respond to large-scale social changes. Ethnography provides an important counter to theoretical extrapolations because it lets us glimpse the local mundane processes which constitute history in the making. It confirms again, that great reform dynamics and people's responses to them must be analysed contextually to show the localised effects of specific histories, institutional practices and cultures.

The principal method of the research was semi-structured and open-ended, in-depth, life history interviewing. In order to contact headteachers and teachers who were experiencing or had experienced stress in their work I collaborated with a local authority Occupational Health Unit which was currently engaged in counselling employees of the local authority (largely teachers, social workers and fire service personnel) who were self-referred, or referred by their General Practitioners and who were experiencing stress. All had been diagnosed as suffering from anxiety, depression or stress-related illness. The Unit also had knowledge of those teachers who had returned to school or who had retired early or otherwise left teaching for stress-related reasons. An operational definition of stress for the research was provided by the criteria of attendance at the Unit for counselling, receiving medical treatment for stress related illness and having a prolonged period off work work. Teachers conforming with this definition were identified by the Unit who circulated our letter to these teachers inviting them to take part in the research. As I obviously was not in a position where I could anticipate, and therefore select, those individuals who would want to co-operate in the research I was reliant on an opportunity sample. Some of the respondents gave me further contacts with friends who were receiving support from the Unit and this provided a small snowball sample.

The eventual sample consisted of twenty teachers, thirteen women and seven men. These worked, or had worked, in schools representing a range of urban and rural locations. The gender proportions and ages in the sample represent those found in the teaching profession generally in that they are predominantly women and a large majority of whom are forty years-old or above (Wragg et al. 1998). A range of positions were represented, though the majority were teachers (mostly subject co-ordinators) in mid to late career. There were three headteachers (two male, one female) and two newly qualified teachers (female). A range of adaptations was evident including teachers on sickness absence, those who had returned to work and some who had left teaching. The teachers who participated were interviewed in their homes. Each interview was normally of one and a half to two hours duration with the length being determined by the interviewee. I had a minimum number of two and a maximum of five interviews with respondents over a two year period. This added a longitudinal dimension to the research, something which is often missing in research on stress in teaching (Kelchtermans, 1995) and enabled me to chart the 'stress career'. Analysis of transcripts, conducted in parallel with ongoing comparisons with related research literature, fed into future interviews and data collection in order to facilitate 'progressive focusing' (Glaser and Strauss, 1967) and an escalation of insights (Lacey, 1976).

Additionally, I conducted an organisational study of two primary schools involving observation and interview. This study was of two large urban primary schools located in different Education Authorities. One was a self-defined 'low stress' school (staffed by a headteacher and eleven class teachers) which had received a highly favourable Ofsted report and had low teacher absence rates; low staff sickness rates; low staff turnover; and high teacher morale. The other, a self-defined 'high stress school', was under 'special measures', having been defined by Ofsted as a 'failing' school. It was experiencing high levels of teacher stress, high staff turnover and high absence rates.

Dissemination and policy

Collaboration with potential 'users' was built into each stage of the research process. The Occupational Health Manager of the Local Authority, where the research was to be located, was approached at the proposal writing stage not only to secure access to a sample of teachers but also for her to comment on the proposed research. We also collaborated with an Assistant Education Officer (Head of Education Personnel) who was a key person in policy formulation for employment health and safety. We discussed our proposal with a clinical psychologist working in a medical school with counsellors of HIV/AIDS and oncology patients. Stress was his principal research interest and he sought to apply quantitative research findings to his work with counsellors. Both the health manager and psychologist acted as referees for the research proposal submitted to the ESRC. The major teachers' trades unions were consulted at the proposal writing stage and in the early phases of the fieldwork. Meetings took place with: the National Association of Schoolmasters and Union of Women Teachers; National Union of Teachers; and Professional Association of Teachers. On such occasions we informed the unions of our research aims and design and discussed ways in which we could support each other in developing the research and ways in which our 'findings' could be fed into their policy making process. These 'users' supported the research because they recognised the potential it had to contribute to policy making in their various areas and in other occupations. The teachers taking part in interviews collaborated with the researcher; some over a two year period involving several interviews. A rather 'unconventional' dissemination of the research took place in many of these interviews as respondents apart from merely answering questions also posed quite a few. They wanted to know, for instance, what we had found out about stress in teaching. They also, in some cases, sought advice on how they could deal with stress in their own work and lives. Thus, we became involved in a form of 'micro-policy making' at this level of dissemination and policy formation and these processes could not, therefore be bracketed off neatly and assigned to the final stage of the research. The motivation for respondents to become involved in the research was various. Some wanted their 'stories' to be told. Some wanted me to publish 'findings' to alert policy makers about the 'reality' of what was happening to teachers and schools. And some wanted to see their stories documented and, through reading, relate their experiences to others in similar circumstances. It is this kind of rapport and respondent 'pressure' which led Lather and Smithies (1997) to desk-top publish their work (Troubling the Angels: Women living with HIV/AIDS) and circulate it to respondents rather than wait for the publisher's slow process to be completed.

Other dissemination included preparing and presenting academic papers at the main educational conferences. Papers were given at the annual conference of the British Educational Research Association; the European Conference on Educational Research; American Educational Research Association; and the Oxford Ethnography and Education conference. Papers and presentations were given at other conferences which included a wide range of disciplines and other occupations and had a mixed audience including academics and non-academics. Such a conference was organised by the United Kingdom National Work-Stress Network News. Papers were circulated to some of the participating teachers for respondent validation. This required writing two versions of the papers. One aimed at a practitioner/policy audience and one for an academic conference audience or journal readership (see Lather, 1997; Richardson, 1990). The health manager and psychologist received copies of papers. Research 'findings' have been used to inform inservice provision for work in schools on teacher stress and an article was published in the practitioner journal Child Education. A one day conference was conducted during the final phase of the research and it was attended by representatives of all of the user groups and all of the teachers participating in the study. A book contract was secured for publication by a major education publishers. This helped disseminate 'findings' nationally and internationally to policy makers, practitioners and academics.

In the stress research we were engaged in social policy research in two senses. Finch (1985, p. 111) explains the two meanings of social policy research as follows:

The first is the academic study of some area where social policies are operating, or perhaps are not operating very effectively. The purpose of such studies is to document and analyse the impact of social policies upon their target populations. The second meaning is, studies conducted with a view to influencing the future direction of the policy; that is, studies which aspire to feed directly into the policy-making process, usually with a view to producing some kind of policy change.

We were concerned with both of these meanings since we were charting some of the effects of policy on the life and work of teachers but also aiming to use research 'findings' to inform policies for the prevention of disabling stress in teachers' work. Our ambition to make policy recommendations as a result of the research involved abandoning naïve conceptions of the relationship between research and policy/practice embodied in the engineering model of educational research. Hammersley (1992, p. 128) describes this as follows:

In its most extreme form the (engineering model) tends to see research as providing sets of policy prescriptions that policy-makers simply have to follow in order to achieve their goals.

While hoping to contribute to knowledge in the discipline of sociology (Hammersley, 1992) we were also operating with the assumptions of the enlightenment model of the research and policy/practice relationship which:

> ... implies a less direct relationship between the knowledge produced and the policies adopted.   (Ibid.)

In the enlightenment model:

> ... the researcher is the provider of knowledge, not just in the sense of 'facts' but, more importantly, of insights which invite participants to reconceptualise their own world and, therefore, possibly to devise ways of changing it.   (Finch, 85, p. 122)

This tradition of social policy research recognises that 'policy can illuminate it cannot dictate' and 'policy research is not social engineering, nor can it aspire to be—it is best suited to enlighten' (Rist, 1984, p. 156 and p. 168).

Any research, like the stress research, which intends to feed research 'findings' into the three policy making contexts (influence, text production, practice) must also be aware of the multiple interpretations 'and effects' (some of them unintended) of social policy and how different readings of policy 'may have very different consequences and implications for practice' (Bowe et al. 1992, p. 23; see also Woods and Wenham, 1995).

The unanticipated ethnographic case study

Burgess (1994, p.58) reminds us that a research 'proposal is a plan about what might occur rather than what should occur'. Departures from the research design stated at the outset in ethnographic projects is highly likely since the ethnographic enterprise centres 'around compromises, short cuts, hunches and serendipitous occurrences' (Walford, 1987, p.1; see also Measor and Woods, 1991 and Woods, 1996b and 1999a). Lee (1993, p. 207) argues that 'researching sensitive topics requires an imaginative cast of mind' and:

> To paraphrase Webb and Weick (1983), foolishness is functional in research. This is not, as might seem at first sight, an invitation to make crass decisions. What Webb and Weick have in mind is that the ability to reflect in an imaginative, playful, even fanciful, way is helpful when

faced with a difficult research situation. Such reflection serves, as they put it, to 'generate novel inputs and permit people to recognise and break the singular focus toward a problem in which they had persisted' (ibid. p. 213). Breaking the 'singular focus' can mean being open to a variety of research strategies. In the case of sensitive topics this makes at least pragmatic sense. Since routes to sensitive data are often blocked, alternative or multiple methods of reaching one's destination often have to be found.

In research of this type it pays to be able to be prepared to use 'any setting in order to examine the unanticipated and respect the complexity of the social world' (Rist, 1984, p. 166).

An opportunity to develop the stress research arose when I discovered in my analysis of the interview data that poor staff relationships were perceived by the teachers to be a major source of stress in their work. One aspect of this was the phenomenon which some participants described as 'bullying'. I also found out that one of the respondents was in the process of setting up a self-help group to support teachers who, like her, considered they had been 'bullied' at work. I later found two more respondents were founder members of this group. These teachers felt they had been, or were being, forced out of teaching and were experiencing stress-related illness and felt marginalised, alienated and powerless. They considered they had been ignored by their trade unions when requesting professional help and support with workplace problems. They, therefore, created an organisation for 'bullied' local authority employees mostly teachers (also some private sector employees) which was designed to give emotional and practical support to colleagues in the network and also publicise their situation, and act as a pressure group devoted to raising these issues with employers and unions; bringing about change in the workplace while seeking redress for their members.

I was invited to join the group as someone who they knew had understanding of and sympathy for their position and who could, potentially, publicise their plight and perhaps influence policy on 'bullying' in the workplace. It was possible for me to attend their monthly evening meetings, at first in a pub and later in a rented hall, and engage in participant observation. This enabled me to conduct the case study in parallel with work on the main project interviewing and school studies. I rregularly attended group meetings for a year and have continued my involvement, , but infrequently since the fieldwork came to a close.

The original proposal and research conducted up to the point of joining the group had been largely on 'conventional' ethnographic lines. While aiming to disseminate research to inform policies which would improve the nature, context and organisation of teachers' work the research did not, at this stage, embody a perspective or rationale derived from critical theory. Working with the group would, it seemed to me, involve engaging in the practice and problematics of critical ethnography which embodies emancipatory ends and:

> ... reflects a movement away from oppressive relations of all kinds— relations that limits peoples' control over their work, denies certain groups access to debates, and obstructs opportunities for a quality life and a movement towards more egalitarian and democratic relations (Gitlin et al. 1993, p. 195) and allows the exploration of social relations and practices of contemporary capitalism as these materialise within the everyday world, whether in schools, hospitals, prisons, gay bars, factories, or coal mines. Second, ethnographic research has a unique capacity to get close up to sites of exploitation and oppression, thereby endowing the researcher with not only first-hand experience of what forms these take and how they are organised but also a privileged standpoint in respect of constructing emancipatory practices (Lather, 1986). For this reason, and its apparent compatibility with a non-positivist epistemology/ontology, ethnography has also been embraced by feminism as a favoured research strategy. (Roberts, 1981; Stanley, 1990)
> (Jordan and Yeomans, 1995, p. 390)

An involvement of this type with the researched would seem to involve not only 'unconventional' ethnography (in being linked to emancipatory projects) but also to problematise notions of relevance, collaboration, 'users' of research, dissemination and policy formation.

There were several opportunities for developing the stress research which presented themselves once I had become part of the group; some of them strongly related to the aims stated in our proposal and research framed by critical theory. Participating in the group presented the opportunities of:

+   learning more about a group of workers who could be considered to be 'deviants'; often the study of 'deviancy' gives insights into 'normalcy' (Woods, 1983);

+   discovering more about the phenomenon of workplace 'bullying' in the workplace as a source of stress;

+ gaining access to teachers and workers in other caring occupations (e.g. social work) who had experienced stress-related illness and had left their jobs or were seriously considering doing so;

+ studying the impact of national, local government and trades union's policies on teachers and other occupational groups;

+ participating in and studying, through a social movement lens (Taylor, 1998), the ideas, policies, organisation, and strategies of a contemporary self-help movement;

+ working with an oppressed group and attempting to conduct research which contributed to social change by making life better for the researched. This could be done by linking critical analysis with social action;

+ if not actually empowering, helping to give a voice to a marginalised and powerless group (Troyna, 1994) who have been 'marginalised or ignored in traditional research' (Taylor, 1998, p. 365);

+ having an opportunity to disseminate my research 'findings' to inform the policies and strategies of the group to support them in their project of achieving policy change nationally, and within the local authority and in their trades unions;

+ being able to put geographically, psychologically and socially isolated participants in the main stress research, who had experienced 'bullying', in contact with a support group.

Although these aims seemed extremely laudable in theory, participation in the work of the group, while researching it, proved to be rather more complex and problematical. I explore some of the issues raised in the context of dissemination for policy use in the following section. I focus on dissemination for policy making within the anti-bullying at work group.

Dissemination for policy making

Dissemination

The anti-bullying group had two main aims; these were supporting colleagues emotionally and psychologically and the political aim of attempting to secure redress from their employers (the local authority) and their unions. The first of these aims was manifest in how meetings were structured and conducted in the early days of the group. At the beginning of meetings members (approximately twenty members attend each meeting) were asked to introduce themselves and say a little about their experiences of being 'bullied' at work. In such sessions members would often refer to themselves as 'victims' or 'targets' of 'bullying' and some talked at length of the trauma of the experience and its aftermath. The chairperson would invite members to 'remind each other of the emotions they had experienced'. Members would respond by 'confirming shared experiences' (Taylor, 1998) and offering advice to each other. All these personal narratives confirmed that members had suffered at the hands of management, commonly a headteacher. I found these 'introduction' phases difficult to sit through because although I had heard many harrowing and emotional stories about bullying from respondents in the stress research I had not experienced this myself and therefore felt uncomfortable as I did not have a tale to tell. There was a tension in the group between those members who had been 'bullied' and those who had not (just myself and two others in this latter group). One female member, who seemed to represent the large majority of the group, felt the group should be uniquely for 'bullied' workers and argued that she 'could not understand the motivations of anyone wanting to come to meetings unless they had experienced 'bullying''. Alternatively one member said she thought it was important to include people who were not 'victims' of 'bullying' because 'they would have a distanced and objective view. All those suffering from "bullying' and stress were so angry —an objective person could disperse some of this anger'.

In the culture of self-reflexivity in late modernity the members used concepts derived from the social sciences in order to explain their situation and reconstruct damaged self identities and mind/body projects (Giddens, 1991). A further aspect of support strategies, therefore, was to provide members with knowledge to aid psychological and physical recovery. To this end they decided to invite 'experts' to speak about aspects of bullying and associated stress. At first the 'experts' were drawn from the group itself. I was invited to give the first talk. I saw this as an opportunity to disseminate some of the research 'findings' which I thought would, by focusing on stress in teaching, support members in helping them to re-contextualise their experience. I chose to talk about sources of stress as perceived by teachers in the study. My theoretical frame was intended to develop macro-meso-micro linkages in explanation of occupational stress. I felt ethnography was a method well suited to this theoretical framework. Like Smith (1987) in developing her methodology of 'institutional ethnography' I felt:

> ... inquiry begins with the work organisation within which individuals are situated, whether as mothers, factory operatives or shop assistants.

It is through the social relations of work we can connect apparently micro-social processes with the wider political economy of contemporary capitalism.   (Jacobs and Yeomans, 1995, p. 398)

The sources of stress I discussed were categorised as follows: the intensification of work; values clash; staff relationships; teacher/pupil relationships; and accountability issues. I made reference to 'bullying' in the section on staff relationships and used examples from my data. I interpreted 'bullying' as a social process and linked the personal experience of it to macro and meso constraints. For example, I cited an explanation used by a leading researcher on stress and 'bullying'. I argued that Cooper (1999) claims the type of psychologically disturbed bully is now relatively rare with the most common form being 'normal' managers who are under pressure to meet targets. There was evidence of 'unconscious managerial bullying' by a manager who experienced accountability pressures which 'led her into putting pressure on others and regretting it, even though she felt it was unavoidable' (Jeffrey and Woods, 1998, p. 126). I pointed out, the Association of Teachers and Lecturers (ATL, 1996) claim that 'bullying' in schools is on the increase and is a major cause of teachers leaving teaching. They hold the cause of this increase to be as follows:

Headteachers in both maintained and independent schools are under enormous pressure to produce results, sometimes within the constraint of very limited resources. This pressure is often passed on to heads of departments or post-holders who are similarly anxious to show that their area is performing well. These stressed managers may find that support and advice are less readily available than in the past and they, in turn, may resort to bullying tactics. Meanwhile, league tables can lead to anxieties that a disappointing showing in a single year will lead to pupils being transferred elsewhere.   (ibid. p. 1)

I indicated that these arguments were supported by sociological research in schools. I cited Reay (1996, p.5) who argues that 'bullying' 'cascades' through the system so that some main grade teachers actually describe themselves as repositories for tensions working their way down through the educational system'. I produced some of my own evidence showing that not all 'bullying' reported to me was carried out by managers. I cited instances of deputy heads being 'bullied' by teachers. And heads being 'bullied' by parents and governors.

After speaking for my allotted thirty minutes the chairperson thanked me and said unfortunately there was no time remaining for questions and a discussion. After the meeting three members remained behind and asked me questions. However, I judged the overall response to the talk was one of non-acceptance of my sociological views on the phenomenon of stress and 'bullying'. I sensed that I had said many things they did not wish to hear.

The following month the group received a talk given by a group member who had recently experienced bullying. Once recovered from his stress-related illness he consulted psychological texts on bullying. In his talk he interpreted 'bullying' in terms of constructing the 'bully' as a 'psychopath' or 'sociopath' who selects 'victims'. They did this, it was argued, because they were inadequate or plain incompetent. The 'serial bully' was defined as having what was described as a 'psychosis' which exhibited the main features of:

Antisocial personality disorder—a pervasive pattern of grandiosity, need for admiration, lack of empathy, exploitative, sense of entitlement, envious, arrogant (example: an overwhelming need to be seen as a kind and caring person).

Paranoid personality disorder—a pervasive distrust and suspiciousness of others such that their motives are interpreted as malevolent, unwilling to confide, unjustified doubts, perceives threats, bears grudges, reacts angrily and counter attacks (example: selecting the person who is competent and popular, choosing to see them as a threat when no threat exists).

A psychopath—is a person who is violent and expresses their violence physically; DSM-IV[1] estimates the prevalence of APD[2] at 1 in 30 for males and 1 in 100 for females. Estimates of prevalence are based almost exclusively on people who are physically violent.

A sociopath—is a person who is violent but due to their high intelligence expresses violence psychologically. I estimate 1 person in 30 (male and female) is a sociopath—possibly more.

Embittered by an abusive upbringing, the serial bully is an individual with a psychotic lack of insight into their behaviour and its effect on others who displays an obsessive, compulsive and self-gratifying urge to displace their uncontrolled aggression onto another person. Jealousy

1. Diagnostic and Statistical Manual of Mental Disorders, Vol. IV, (1994) Washington: American Psychiatric Association.
2. Antisocial Personality Disorder

and envy impel the bully to identify a competent and popular individual who the bully then controls and subjugates through projection of inadequacy and incompetence. When the target asserts their right not to be bullied, a paranoid fear of exposure compels the bully to perceive that person as a threat and thus dispose of them as quickly as possible.

(notes from the handout distributed at the talk)

At key moments throughout his talk on the psychological characteristics of the 'bully' he would pause and say 'do you recognise this?' and 'is this familiar to you?'. The group members, by nervous laughs, nodding and verbal acknowledgement, frequently assured him that this was true of their knowledge of 'bullies'. One member said 'he had not fully understood what was happening to him until he had read the book' on which the talk was based. At the conclusion of the talk time was devoted to questions and discussion. There were many questions asked but no member challenged the speaker's theorisation of bullying or construction of the 'bully'. They were all either seeking advice from him on strategies they could use to deal with a 'bullying' manager or how to seek justice through an industrial tribunal, for example.

Following this experience it was quite clear to me that the majority of the group held an interpretation of 'bullying' which was at odds with my own. There is nothing unique in this. Taylor (1998, p. 365) argues that researching social movements requires the researcher to 'listen to and hear voices unlike one's own'. Lee (1993, p. 210) argues that the 'researcher is often a disappointment to the people he or she studies'. This is because researchers 'feel committed to their discipline which often makes them less attracted to the views of those they study than research participants would like' (ibid.). Other researchers have noted the popularity of 'psychologised views' to explain phenomena which are 'strongly at variance with those of sociologists' (ibid.). I was concerned, however, that the individualisation of 'bullying' and the creation of a 'cult of victimisation' (Taylor, 1998) was not only potentially disempowering for the group but if reported in the public domain (by myself or group members) would lead to 'victim blaming' taking place. There can be a tendency in situations where 'victims' rely on individualised interpretations to account for their plight to give legitimacy to these kind of explanations as Finch (1985) has argued. This is supported by the stress research with the example of a female respondent who was being 'bullied' at work and also at home by a violent partner. When she sought professional help with this situation her G.P. asked 'what do you think it is it about you that attracts bullies into your life?'. All the 'victimology literature does is to inform us victims are victimised because they are victims' (Marais-Steinman, 1999). Blaming the victim is a potential of some kinds of stress research which by individualising the 'problem' in utilising personality theory, for instance, raise questions which focus on what are viewed as individual fallibility's rather than exploring wider contextual factors. This issue was raised on an Internet discussion list on anti-bullying topics:

> The worst case scenario is that academic-based researchers could be alienated from experience-based researchers and targets when they are perceived to be coldly intellectualising without real understanding and empathy for the target and the other way round when the experienced-based researchers and targets are perceived to be intolerant when the bully is viewed anything more than an incurable sub-human. This would be a sad day and damage our cause and we should guard against creating such perceptions wittingly or unwittingly.
>
> (Liefooghe, 1999)

Finch (1985) rather than focusing on 'individual patterns of behaviour which might be characterised by readers as 'pathological began to consider more fully the structural arrangements surrounding the lives of those she studied' (Lee, 1993, p. 193). Lee (ibid.) comments that:

> Felson (1991) argues that the kind of strategy Finch adopts is a recurrent one in sociology. The difficulty is, he argues, that in trying to avoid blaming the victim researchers ignore what he terms proximate variables and mediating processes. Instead they typically prefer structural explanations based on the analysis of exogenous variables. Conventional sociological analysis, according to Felson, therefore, exhibits an ambivalent attitude towards explanations which invoke socialisation. It emphasises, by contrast, constraints which affect the lives of subordinate group members as well as their mistreatment at the hands of the powerful. Felson is probably correct to attack what has sometimes seemed like a rather glib sociologising of social problems but there seems no reasons why disciplines like sociology should not provide a corrective to views based on cultural or psychological determinism, and which are already well-entrenched in the wider society. Furthermore, by proximate

variables Felson seems to mean variables of an essentially psycho-logistic kind. It is true that such variables have, by and large, been ignored by sociologists. This is because, more often, they have preferred to explore the proximate bases of behaviour in a dynamic way through case-based methods, ethnography or community study. It is these methods, rather than theoretical predilections, which have frequently demonstrated very clearly how structural factors are massively implicated in everyday life.

The group members views of the sources and nature of their oppression could be dismissed as false consciousness (Sharp, 1982, Mills, 1959). However I was loathe to do this since this would involve adopting an 'Olympian position' (Hammersley, 1981) in which I claimed to have privileged access to a version of reality which was denied to the researched. I do not know, and have no means of knowing, if their perspectives on their oppression was as a result of distortions produced by capitalist hegemonic ideology. Alternatively, I explained their apparent reluctance to re-contextualise their experience in terms of their stress-related illness. All of the members had experienced extremely traumatic experiences (some were being treated for post-traumatic stress disorder and some for depression) and it was fairly clear to me that they were unable to distance themselves from the emotionally painful events which had caused their work-related illness. This reaction to stressful work was certainly borne out by data in the main stress research where respondents reported being withdrawn and intensely introspective during their illness. Thus, inability to depersonalise situations (Matza and Sykes, 1957) made socially de-contextualised and psychologised explanations of bullying (such as the psychologised version discussed above) attractive to them. Perhaps, given time for recovery and healing, the members would be able to locate their experience in wider social structural explanations. As Jacobs and Yeomans (1995, p. 401) explain, 'making the world problematic for ourselves is not enough' making it problematic for participants in the research is, in critical ethnography, the point.

Of course, the situation might have called for a different kind of dissemination. My presentation had been in the form of a traditional conference paper albeit revised for a non-academic audience. An alternative form of presentation and representation in which the 'sociology was heavily implicit but not stated in traditional terms' (Woods, 1999c). Such forms have been termed 'performance texts' by Denzin, (1997). The performance text is a:

... genre within ethnography, what Paget (1993) calls ethnoperformance, Mienczakowski (1994) labels ethnodrama, and Turner (1982, p. 41) terms performance and reflexive anthropology, the rendering 'of ethnography in a kind of instructional theatre' (Turner, 1982, p. 41).

(Denzin, 1997, p. 91).

Performance texts;

turn tales of suffering, loss, pain and victory into evocative performances that have the ability to move audiences to reflective critical action and not just emotional catharsis ... they can undo the voyeuristic gaze of the ethnographer, bringing audiences and performers into a jointly shared field of experience. These works also unsettle the writer's place in the text, freeing the text and the writer to become interactional productions. The performance text is the single, most powerful way for ethnography to recover yet interrogate the meanings of lived experience.

(ibid. pp. 94-95).

Policy making

My continuing involvement with the group had implications for disseminating research for policy making at local and national levels.

Every ethnographer at some stage in the research will face a 'trust test' (Wolcott, 1995) from members of the culture being researched. This occurred to me when the group had managed to secure a meeting with the Chief Education Officer and Head of Personnel in order to discuss the issue of the 'bullying' of teachers in the local authority. The three members comprising the delegation intended to 'confront' these representatives of the local authority with evidence of the extent and nature of 'bullying'. I was approached to act as a note taker for the meeting. I felt that my commitment and loyalty to the group was under test but felt it necessary to refuse their request. Although I would have had an opportunity of observing and, perhaps, participating in the local policy making process I felt attendance would compromise my position as an 'objective' researcher within the local authority. I had negotiated access, it will be remembered, to teachers for the main research with the Head of Personnel and since she was to be at the meeting I did not want things to appear as though I had sided with the marginalised group of 'bullied' teachers. Since I would eventually be making a report containing policy recommendations to the local authority I did not want it to appear that I would be producing an 'underdog' account (Gouldner, 1968). I thought that she would feel that this would be no basis on which to form policy. Thus the alleged relativism of ethnographic accounts (Hammersley, 1992; 1994) looked an unpromising foundation for policy. I explained this to the delegation and suggested they find some 'demonstrably neutral' person who could act as a note taker.

Another opportunity to influence policy arose when a group member (also a trade union official) approached the Health and Safety Executive (HSE) who were conducting a 'stress audit' on stress amongst local authority employees. This survey would also influence HSE policy at national level. The member asked if I could provide him with any articles arising from my work with teachers in the authority. He intended to give a summary of the paper at his meeting with the representative of the HSE. While I was encouraged that the representation of a teachers' union had in the past informed HSE policy on stress considerably, I had several concerns which were as follows:

- the paper represented work in progress and would, I felt, be an unsuitable basis for policy making;
- the group member was requesting numbers of cases of bullying in the authority—information I did not have;
- there were issues surrounding the confidentiality of some of the data;
- I had read research reports commissioned by the HSE and they were wholly positivistic and quantitative. I also was aware of the survey methodology in their own stress 'audit' work. I, therefore, thought that a qualitative study of teacher stress might lack credibility in their eyes.

While he had a copy of the paper, I suggested he did not use it as the basis of his evidence for the above reasons.

Conclusion

These two examples reveal something of the tension which exists in the researchers' role between, on the one hand, engagement in 'conventional' ethnography, and on the other, 'critical' ethnography. In the role of 'conventional' ethnographer I seek to inform policies by disseminating research products created using methodologies which incorporate safeguards attempting to secure 'objectivity' and 'validity'. As the critical ethnographer I am required to raise/ change the consciousness of participants then fight their corner. In engaging in research as praxis while also conducting a 'conventional' ethnographic study involves magnifying the already stressful tension between researcher involvement and distance (Woods, 1996). Which is, no doubt, why some (Gitlin et al. 1993; Lather, 1986), advocate abandoning the 'conventional' in favour of the 'critical' approach.

I felt that my experience of dissemination for policy making with the anti-bullying group, while getting off to an unpromising start has subsequently contributed to the main research considerably; particularly in the area of dissemination and policy making.

Without becoming a member of the group I would not have come to know the extent of the 'bullying' problem or what it was like to experience the phenomenon. I would also not have learned that the policies of trades unions and local authorities were not, in the opinion of participants, serving some members/employees interests. For example, many trades union members who were facing competency procedures (often in their view, involving 'bullying') were not, in their view, being supported by their unions. Additionally, it was clear that the local authority's policies on stress in the workplace needed the inclusion of policy and procedures concerning 'bullying'. Both of these issues will obviously inform future dissemination for policy making. Informing powerful groups of issues such as these may, however, make sociologists 'unpopular' with policy makers for as Woods and Pollard (1988, p. 11) argue:

> ... when particular concentrations of wealth or power are revealed, or when speeches and policies are analysed in terms of their ideologies and interests which they serve, some people or groups may feel threatened and may seek to discount, neutralise or undermine the source of the analysis.

Being a member of the group has enabled new dissemination opportunities for policy making. For instance, I have been contacted by a Labour Peer who was introducing a 'fairness at work bill'. I have also been consulted by two television producers involved in making programmes on stress and 'bullying' at work.

Like Woods (1999b, p. 18) I see 'enormous possibilities' for ethnographic research at present and in the future however much of these 'run alongside overbearing constraints'. The focus of the research was very much a 'hot' topic. This was reflected in the subsequent Cabinet Office inquiry (1998) into 'Managing Attendance in the Public Sector' and research areas prioritised by the DfEE (Education, 1999), for example, 'Ill health retirement and absenteeism amongst teachers', and 'Factors contributing to teacher effectiveness'. We consider, therefore, that our research was a timely contribution to policy making in these areas.

In the unanticipated 'departure' from the main project I have encountered many of the considerable philosophical and methodological problems foreshadowed by Hammersley (1992; 1994). However, my continuing involvement with the group enables me to feed knowledge gained in the stress research into group decisions and strategies. But this phase of reflection and action was likely to take me considerably beyond the comparatively short timescale of the funded research. The real impact of the research on policy may benefit teachers of the future rather the ones that participated in the research.

In terms of 'overbearing constraints', Jordan and Yeomans (1995, p. 404) argue that all forms of qualitative research must be carried out in 'unfavourable circumstances':

We must acknowledge that current developments in education in both North America and Britain provide an unpromising context for the development of critical, or indeed conventional forms of action research and ethnography. The intensification of teachers' work and tightening control over the curriculum has been well documented e.g. Ball (1994), Apple (1988; 1989; 1993), A. Hargreaves (1993). Academic researchers also face many difficulties; increased pressure from funding bodies for research which is 'relevant' to 'users'; invitations to carry out 'conformative evaluations' of self styled 'innovative' programmes (Stronach and Morris, 1994); pressure from within institutions to secure funding in a highly competitive environment and publish research results in order to promote 'performance' in research assessment exercises; the continued and growing use of research staff on short-term contracts; increasing teaching and administrative workloads. These conditions provide a powerful set of material constraints on researchers.

References

Acker, S. (1990) Teachers' Culture in an English Primary School: continuity and change, *British Journal of Sociology of Education*, 11(3): 257-273.

Aggleton, P. (1987) *Rebels without a cause*, Lewes: Falmer.

Alexander, R., Rose. J. and Woodhead, C. (1992) *Curriculum Organisation and Classroom Practice in Primary Schools: a discussion paper*, London: Department of Education and Science.

Alvesson, M. and Deetz, S. (2000) *Kritisksamhällsvetenskaplig metod*, Lund: Studentlitteratur.

Apple, M. (1986) *Teachers and Texts*, London: Routledge and Kegan Paul.

Apple, M. (1988) Social crisis and curriculum accords, *Educational Theory*, 38: 191-201.

Apple, M. (1989) *Teachers and Texts*, London: Routledge and Kegan Paul.

Apple, M. (1993) *Official Knowledge: Democratic education in a Conservative age*, New York: Routledge.

Arnstberg, K. (1997) *Etnologiskt fältmetodik*, Stockholm: Karlsons.

Ash, R. (1988) *The Impressionnists and their Art*, London: MacDonald.

Association of Teachers and Lecturers (1996) *Bullying at Work: a Guide for Teachers*, London: London: ATL

Atkinson, P. (1990) *The Ethnographic Imagination, Textual Construction of Reality*, London: Routledge.

Ball, S. J. (1981) *Beachside comprehensive*, Cambridge: Cambridge University Press.

Ball, S. J. (1983) Case study research in education: some notes and problems, in: M. Hammersley (ed.) *The Ethnography of Schooling*, Driffield: Nafferton.

Ball, S. J. (1984) Beachside reconsidered: reflections on a methodological apprenticeship, in: R. G. Burgess (ed.) *The Research Process in Educational Settings: ten case studies*, Lewes: Falmer Press.

Ball, S. J. (1988) Staff relations during the teachers' industrial action: context, conflict and proletarianisation, *British Journal of Sociology of Education*, Vol. 9, pp. 289-306.

Ball, S. J. (1990a) Self-doubt and soft data; social and technical trajectories in ethnographic fieldwork, *Qualitative Studies in Education*, 3: 157-171.

Ball, S. J. (1990b) *Politics and Policy Making in Education: explorations in policy sociology*, London: Routledge.

Ball, S. J. (1994) *Education Reform: A critical and post-structural approach*, Buckingham: Open University Press.

Ball, S. J. (2000) Performativities and fabrications in the education economy: Towards the performative society? *Australian Educational Researcher*, 27(2): 1-23.

Ball, S. J. (2003) *Class Strategies and the Education Market: The middle classes and social advantage*, London: Routledge Falmer.

Ball, S.J. (1987) *The Micro-Politics of the School: Towards a theory of school organisation*, London: Methuen.

Barthes, R. (1977) *Image Music Text*, New York, Hill and Wang.

Bassey, M. (1998) Turmoil and Opportunity, Research Intelligence, *British Educational Research Association Newsletter*, October, 66: 1.

Beach, D. (1995) *Making Sense of the Problems of Change: An Ethnographic Study of a Teacher Education Reform*, (Göteborg Studies in Educational Research 100) Göteborg: Acta Universitatis Gothoburgensis,.

Beach, D. (1997) *Symbolic Control and Power Relay: Learning in Higher Professional Education.* (Göteborg Studies in Educational Research 119) Göteborg: Acta Universitatis Gothoburgensis.

Beach, D. (2000) Continuing problems of teacher education reform. *Scandinavian Journal of Educational Research,* 44(3): 275-291.

Beach, D. (2000) Researching Practices through Reflective Conversations on the Value of Research: An Allegory on Forms of Knowledge and a Form of Struggle. Paper presented at the *Making a Difference through Reflective Practices: Values and Actions Conference,* Worcester University College, England, July.

Bengtsson, J. (1993) *Sammanflätningar. Husserls och Merleau-Pontys fenomenologi,* Göteborg: Daidalos.

Berger, P. L. (1966) *Invitation to Sociology,* New York: Doubleday.

Beynon, J. (1983) Ways-in and Staying-in': fieldwork as problem solving, in: M. Hammersley (ed.) *The Ethnography of Schooling,* Driffield: Nafferton.

Black, P. (1993) The shifting scenery of the National Curriculum, in: Chitty, C. and Simon, B. (eds) *Education Answers Back; critical responses to government policy,* London: Lawrence and Wishart.

Bleakley, A. (2000) The refracted practitioner: clinical judgement in medicine under conditions of uncertainty, uniqueness and value conflict. Paper presented at the *Making a Difference through Reflective Practices: Values and Actions,* conference, July 13-16, Worcester University College, Worcester, U.K.

Blumer, H. (1969) *Symbolic Interactionism. Perspective and Method,* Englewood Cliffs: Prentice Hall International.

Blumer, H. (1976) The methodological position of symbolic interactionism, in Hammersley, M. and Woods, P. (eds) *The Process of Schooling,* London, Routledge and Kegan Paul.

Blumer, H. Hauser, P. (1933) *Movies, Delinquency and Crime,* New York: Macmillan

Borgnakke, K. (1996) *Processanalytisk teori og metode: Binde 1 og 2,* Copenhagen: Danish University Press.

Bourdieu, P. (1996) *The Rules of Art: Genesis and Structure of the Literary Field,* Cambridge: Polity Press.

Bowe, R., Ball, S. J. with Gold, A. (1992) *Reforming Education and Changing Schools: Case Studies in Policy Sociology,* London: Routledge.

Britzman, D. P. (1995) The question of belief: writing poststructural ethnography, *International Journal of Qualitative Studies in Education,* 8(3): 229-238.

Brown, M. and Ralph, S. (1998) Change-Linked Stress in British Teachers, paper presented to the British Educational Research Association Conference, Queen's University Belfast.

Bruner, J. (1990) *Acts of Meaning,* Cambridge: Harvard University Press.

Bruner, J. (1996) *The Culture of Education,* Cambridge: Harvard University Press.

Burgess, R. G. (1994) Scholarship and Sponsored Research: Contradiction, Continuum or Complimentary Activity?, in Halpin, D. and Troyna, B. (eds) *Researching Education Policy: ethical and methodological issues,* London: Falmer Press.

Burgess, R. G. (ed.) (1984) *The Research Process in Educational Settings: ten case studies,* Lewes: Falmer Press.

Burgess, R.G. (1983) *Experiencing comprehensive education,* London: Tavistock.

Cabinet Office (1998) *Working Well Together: Managing Attendance in the Public Sector,* London: Cabinet Office.

Campbell, R. J., Evans, L., St. J. Neill, S. R., and Packwood, A. (1991) The use and management of infant teachers' time-some policy issues, paper presented at *Policy Analysis Unit Seminar*, Warwick, November.

Campbell, R. J., Evans, L., St. J. Neill, S. R. and Packwood, A. (1992) The impact of educational reform on infant teachers' work and their perceptions of work, paper prepared for *CEDAR International Conference*, University of Warwick.

Campbell, R. J., Evans, L., St. J. Neill, S. R. and Packwood, A. (1993) *The Use and Management of Infant Teachers' Time: some policy issues*, Stoke-on-Trent: Trentham Books.

Campbell, R.J. (1988) Conflict and strain in the postholder's role, in Glatter, R., Preedy, M., Riches, C. and Masterson, M. (eds) *Understanding School Management*, Milton Keynes: Open University Press.

Campbell, R. J. and St. J. Neill, S. R. (1994) *Curriculum Reform at Key Stage 1: Teacher Commitment and Policy Failure*, Harlow: Longman.

Carr, W. (1987) What is an Educational Practice?, *Journal of Philosophy of Education*, 22(2): 163 -175.

Carspecken, P. (1991) *Community schooling and the nature of power*, London: Routledge.

Clifford, J and Marcus, G. (1986) *Writing Culture: The Poetics and Politics of Ethnography*, Berkeley: University of California Press.

Clifford, J. (1986b) On ethnographic allegory, in Clifford, J. and Marcus, G. (1986) *Writing Culture: The Poetics and Politics of Ethnography*, Berkeley: University of California Press.

Clifford, J. (1990) On ethnographic fieldnotes, in Sanjek, R. (ed.) *Fieldnotes—The Makings of Anthropology* , Ithaca and London: University of Cornell Press.

Clough, P. C. (2000) Comments on setting criteria for experimental writing, *Qualitative Inquiry*, 6(2): 278-291.

Cooper, C. (1999) We must deny bullies a pulpit, *Times Higher Education Supplement*, Friday 23rd April.

Cooper, P. and McIntyre, D. (1996) *Effective Teaching and Learning*, Milton Keynes: Open University Press.

Corrigan, P. (1979) *Schooling and the Smash Street Kids*, London: MacMillan.

Cunningham, P. (1988) *Curriculum Change in the Primary School since 1945: dissemination of the progressive ideal*, Lewes: Falmer Press.

Dale, R. (1992) Recovering from a pyrrhic victory? Quality, relevance and impact in the sociology of education, in: Arnot, M. and Barton, L. (eds) *Voicing Concerns: sociological perspectives on contemporary education reforms*, Wallingford: Triangle Books.

Davies, B. and R. Harre, R. (1994) Positioning, Conversation and the Production of Selves. *Journal for the Theory of Social Behaviour* 20(1): 43-63.

Delamont, S. (1984) The old girl network: reflections on the fieldwork at St Luke's, in: Burgess, R. G. (ed.) *The Research Process in Educational Settings: ten case studies*, Lewes: Falmer Press.

Denzin N. K. and Lincoln, Y. S. (1998) Collecting and interpreting qualitative materials, in Denzin N. K. and Lincoln, Y. S. (eds), *Handbook of qualitative research paperback, edition 3*, London: Sage Publications.

Denzin, N. K (1994) The Art and Politics of Interpretation, in Denzin, N. K. and Lincoln, Y. S. (eds) *Handbook of Qualitative* Research, London: Sage.

Denzin, N. K. (1978) *The Research Act*, New York: McGraw Hill.

Denzin, N. K. (1997) *Interpretive Ethnography: Ethnographic Practices for the 21st Century*, Thousand Oaks: SAGE.

Denzin, N. K. (2000) Aesthetics and the practices of qualitative inquiry, *Qualitative Inquiry*, 6(2):256-265.

Denzin, N. K. and Lincoln, Y. S. (1994) Introduction: Entering the field of qualitative research, in Denzin, N. and Lincoln, Y (eds.) *Handbook of Qualitative Research*, London and New York: Sage.

Department of Education and Science (1992) *Curriculum Organisation and Classroom Practice in Primary Schools: A Discussion Paper*, London: DES Information Branch.

Derrida, J. (1976) *Of Grammatology*, Balitimore: John Hopkins University Press.

Derrida, J. (1981) Structure, sign and play in the discoure of the human sciences, in Derrida, J. *Writing and Difference*, London: Routledge and Kegan Paul.

Derrida, J. (1991) *Cinders*, Lincoln, U.S.A. and London: University of Nebraska Press.

Derrida, J (1994) *Spectres of Marx: The State of the Debt, the Work of Mourning and the New International*, Routledge: London.

Driessen, H. (1993) (ed.) *The Politics of Ethnographic Reading and Writing: Confrontrations of Western and Indigenous Views*, Verlag: Breitenbach Publishers.

Education Journal (1999) DfEE Research, *Education Journal*, May: 31-32.

Ellis, C. (2000) Creating criteria: an ethnographic short story, *Qualitative Inquiry*, 6(2):273-277.

Erickson, F. (1986) *Qualitative methods in research on teaching, in: M. C. Wittock (ed.) Handbook of Research on Teaching*, New York, Macmillan.

ESRC (1987) *A New Structure for The Economic and Social Research Council*, London: ESRC.

Evans, L., Packwood, A., St. J. Neill, S. R. and Campbell, R. J. (1994) *The Meaning of Infant Teachers' Work*, London: Routledge.

Fay, B. (1977) *Social Theory and Political Practice*, London: George Allen and Unwin.

Felson, R. B. (1991) Blame Analysis: Accounting for the Behavior of Protected Groups, *American Sociologist*, 22: 5-23.

Filer, A. and Pollard, A. (2000) *The Social World of Pupil Assessment*, London: Continuum Books.

Finch, J. (1985) Social Policy and Education: problems and possibilities of using qualitative research, in Burgess, R. (ed.) *Issues in Educational Research: Qualitative Methods*, Lewes: Falmer.

Fitz, J., Halpin, D. and Power, S. (1994) Implementation Research and Education Policy: practice and prospects, *British Journal of Educational Studies*, 42(1): 53-69.

Flude, M. and Hammer, M. (1990) *The Education Reform Act 1988: its origins and implications*, Basingstoke: Falmer Press.

Foucault, M. (1977) *Discipline and Punish: The birth of the prison*. London: Penguin.

Fullan, M. (1988) Change process in secondary schools: towards a more fundamental agenda, University of Toronto (mimeo).

Garfinkle, H. (1967) *Studies in Ethnomethodology*, Englewood-Cliffs: Prentice-Hall.

Geertz, C. (1973) Thick description: toward an interpretive theory of culture in Geertz, C. (ed.) *The Interpretation of Cultures: selected essays by Clifford Geertz*, New York, Basic Books.

Geertz, C. (1973) *The Interpretation of Cultures*, New York: Basic Books.

Geertz, C. (1983) *Local Knowledge*, New York: Basic Books.

Genosko, G. (1994) *Baudrillard and Signs: Signification Ablaze*, London: Routledge.

Gewirtz, S., Ball, S. J. and Bowe, R. (1995) *The Managerial School: Post-Welfarism and Social Justice in Education*, London: Routledge.

Giddens, A. (1987) *The Constitution of Society*, Cambridge: Polity Press.

Giddens, A. (1991) *Modernity and Self-Identity*, Cambridge: Polity.

Gillborn, D. (1994) The Micro-politics of Macro Reform, *British Journal of Sociology of Education*, 15(2): 147-164.

Gipps, C. (1993) Policy-making and the use and misuse of evidence, in: Chitty, C. and Simon, B. (eds) *Education Answers Back: critical responses to government policy*, London: Lawrence and Wishart.

Giroux, H. (1981) Ideology, *Culture and the Process of Schooling, Philadelphia*, Philadelphia: Temple University Press.

Gitlin A., Bringhurst, M., Burns, M., Cooley, V., Myers, B., Price, K., Russell, R. Tiess, P. (1992) *Teachers' Voices for School Change: an introduction to educative research*, London: Routledge.

Gitlin, A. Siegel, M. and Boru, K. (1993) The Politics of Method: from leftist ethnography to educative research, in Hammersley, M. (ed.) *Educational Research: Current Issues*, London: Paul Chapman.

Glaser, B. G. and Strauss, A. L. (1967) *The Discovery of Grounded Theory: strategies for qualitative research*, Chicago: Aldine.

Glazer, M. (1972) *The Research Adventure: promise and problems of fieldwork*, New York: Random House.

Goffman, E. (1961) *Asylums*, Harmondsworth: Penguin.

Goffman, I. (1959) *The Presentation of Self in Everyday Life*, London: Penguin.

Gomm, R., Foster, P. and Hammersley, M. (1998) Case Study and Generalisation, paper presented to the *Case Study Research in Education Conference, CEDAR*, University of Warwick, March.

Gouldner, A. W. (1968) The Sociologist as Partisan, *American Sociologist*, May: 103-116.

Grace, G. (1995) School Leadership: *Beyond Education Management, An Essay in Policy Scholarship*, London: Falmer Press.

Granath, G. (1999) *Redo för fronten? Ett reportage från lärarhögskolan*, Stockholm: Ordfront Förlag.

Green, J.L. and Miller, H.D.R. (1999) Universities and the Academic Labour Process, Cases and Reflections, paper presented at the *17th Annual International Labour Process Conference*, Royal Holloway College, University of London, March.

Grossberg, L. (1996) Identity and cultural studies-Is that all there is? in Hall, S. and Du Gay, P. (eds) *Questions of Cultural Identity*. London: Sage Publications.

Guba, E. G. and Lincoln, Y. S. (1994) Competing paradigms in qualitative research, in Denzin, N. and Lincoln, Y (eds) *Handbook of Qualitative Research*, London: Sage.

Gubrium, J. F. and Holstein, J. A. (1997) *The New Language of Qualitative Method*, Oxford: Oxford University Press.

Habenstein, R.W. (1970) *Pathways to Data*, Chicago: Aldine.

Hall, S. and Jefferson, T. (1978) (eds) *Resistance Through Rituals*, London:Hutchinson.

Halpin, D. and Troyna, B. (eds) (1994) *Researching Education Policy: ethical and methodological issues*, London: Falmer Press.

Hammersely, M. (1992) *What's Wrong With Ethnography*, London: Routledge

Hammersley, M. (1980) On Interactionist Empiricism, in Woods, P. (ed.) *Pupil Strategies: Explorations in the Sociology of the School*, London: Croom Helm.

Hammersley, M. (1981) Ideology in the Staffroom? A Critique of False Consciousness, in Barton, L. and Walker, S. (eds) *Schools, Teachers and Teaching*, Lewes: Falmer Press.

Hammersley, M. (1984) The Researcher exposed: a natural history, in: R. G. Burgess (ed.) *The Research Process in Educational Settings: ten cases studies*, Lewes; Falmer Press.

Hammersley, M. (1992) *Reading Ethnographic Research: A Critical Guide*, London: Longmann.

Hammersley, M. (1992) *What's wrong with Ethnography?*, London:Routledge.

Hammersley, M. (1993) Is research political? paper prepared for *Economic and Social Research Council Sponsored Seminar* on Methodology and Epistemology in Educational Research, University of Liverpool, June. .

Hammersley, M. (1994) Ethnography, Policy Making and Practice in Education, in Halpin, D. and Troyna, B. (eds) *Researching Education Policy: ethical and methodological issues*, London: Falmer Press.

Hammersley, M. (1996) *Educational Research in Action, E835 Study Guide*, Milton Keynes: The Open University

Hammersley, M. (ed.) (1983) *The Ethnography of Schooling*, Driffield: Nafferton.

Hammersley, M. and Atkinson, P. (1983/1995) *Ethnography: principles in practice*, London: Tavistock.

Hammersley, M. and Scarth, J. (1993) Beware of wise men bearing gifts: a case study in the misuse of educational research, *British Educational Research Journal*, 19: 489-498.

Hammersley, M., Gomm. R. and Foster, P. (1998) Case Study and Theory, paper presented to the *Case Study Research in Education Conference, CEDAR*, University of Warwick, March.

Hannertz, U. (1969) *Soulside*, New York: Columbia University Press.

Hargreaves, A. (1980) Synthesis and the Study of Strategies: a project for the sociological imagination' in Woods, P. (ed.) *Pupil Strategies: explorations in the sociology of the school*, London: Croom Helm.

Hargreaves, A. (1984) Marxism and Relative Autonomy, Unit 22 in Course E205 *Conflict and Change in Education*, Milton Keynes: Open University.

Hargreaves, A. (1985) The Micro-Macro Problem in the Sociology of Education, in Burgess, R. G. (ed.) *Issues in Educational Research: Qualitative Methods*, Lewes: Falmer Press.

Hargreaves, A. (1986) The micro-macro problem in the sociology of education, in: Hammersley, M. (ed.) *Controversies in Classroom Research*, Milton Keynes: Open University Press.

Hargreaves, A. (1993) Time and teachers' work: an analysis of the intensification thesis, in Gomm, R. and Woods, P. (eds) *Educational Research in Action*, London: Paul Chapman.

Hargreaves, A. (1994) *Changing Teachers. Changing Times: teachers' work and culture in the postmodern age*, London: Cassell.

Hargreaves, A. (1998) Review Symposium, *British Journal of Sociology of Education*, 19(3): 419-423.

Hargreaves, D. H. (1996) *Teaching as a research based profession: possibilities and prospects*, Teacher Training Agency Annual Lecture.

Hargreaves, D.H. (1967) *Social Relations in the Secondary School*, London: Routledge and Kegan Paul.

Harris, P. (1995) Learning to Manage: changing jobs, changing selves?, paper presented at the *Annual Labour Process Conference*, Blackpool, April.

Harrison, S., Hunter, D. and Marnoch, G. (1992) *Just Managing: Power and Culture in the National Health Service*, Basingstoke: Macmillan.

Hayes, D (1994) Teachers' Involvement in Decision-Making: a case study of a primary school at a time of rapid change, Unpublished PhD. Thesis, University of Plymouth.

Held, D. (1980) *Introduction to Critical Theory*, London: Hutchinson.

Hellawell, D. (1990) Some effects of the national dispute on relationships between headteachers and school staffs in primary schools, *British Journal of Sociology of Education*, 11: 397-410.

Helmstad, G. (1999) *Understandings of Understanding: An Inquiry Concerning Experiential Conditions for Developmental Learning*, (Göteborg Studies in Educational Science 134), Göteborg: Acta Universitatis Gothoburgensis.

Hillage, J., Pearson, R., Anderson, A. and Tamkin, P. (1998) *Excellence in Research on Schools*, London: Department for Education and Employment.

Hirst, P. H. (1983) *Educational Theory and its Foundation Disciplines*, London:Routledge and Kegan Paul.

Hitchcock, G. and Hughes, D. (1989) *Research and the Teacher: a Qualitative Introduction to School-based Research*, London: Routledge.

Horkheimer, M. (1974) *Critique of Instrumental Reason*, New York: Seabury.

Hoyle, E. (1974) Professionalility, professionalism and control in teaching, *London Educational Review*, 3(2): 15-17, also (1975) in Houghton, V., McHugh, R. and Morgan, C. (eds) *Management in Education: The Management of Organizations and Individuals*, London: Ward Lock Educational in Association with the Open University Press.

Hughes, E. C. (1960) Introduction: the place of field work in social science, in: B. Junker (ed.) *An Introduction to the Social Sciences*, Chicago: University of Chicago Press.

Hughes, M. G. (1985) Leadership in professionally staffed organisations, in: Hughes, M. G., Ribbins, P. and Thomas, H. (eds) *Managing Education: the system and the institution*, London: Holt, Rinehart and Winston.

Jeffrey B. (forthcoming). How to 'describe' ethnographic research sites. in Gobbo, F. (ed.) *Etnografia dell'educazione in Europa*, Mila: Edizioni Unicopli.

Jeffrey, B. (1994) Changing Identities: The case of the primary teacher in Late Modernity. *Paper presented at AERA*, New Orleans.

Jeffrey, B. (1995). Problematising conversations. Paper read at *Ethnography Conference* at St Hilda's at Warwick.

Jeffrey, B. (1997) Framing creativity in primary classrooms, in *Can you teach creativity*, edited by A. Craft. Nottingham: Education Now.

Jeffrey, B. (1999) Sidestepping the Substantial Self: The fragmentation of primary teacher's self through audit accountability, in Hammersley. M. (ed) *Researching School Experience: Ethnographic Studies of Teaching and Learning*, London: Falmer.

Jeffrey, B. (1999) Distancing research objects through the involvement of the self, in Massey, A. W. Walford, G. (eds.) *Studies in educational ethnography: explorations in ethnography*, Stamford Connecticut: Jai Press.

Jeffrey, B. (2000) Challenging prescription in ideology and practice: the case of Sunny first school, in *Understanding Pedagogy*, Collins, J., Insley, K. and Craft, A. (eds.) Buckingham: Open University Press.

Jeffrey, B. (2002) Performativity and changing teacher relations. *Journal of Educational Policy.* 17(5): 531-546.

Jeffrey, B. (2003) Countering student instrumentalism: A creative response. *British Educational Research Journal.* 29(4)

Jeffrey, B. and Woods, P. (1998) *Testing Teachers: The Effect of School Inspections on Primary Teachers*, London: Falmer Press.

Jordan, S. and Yeomans, D. (1995) Critical Ethnography: problems in contemporary theory and practice, *British Journal of Educational Studies*, 16(3): 389-408.

Junker, B. (1960) *Fieldwork* , Chicago: University of Chicago Press.

Kanepalli Kanth, R. (1999), *Breaking with the Enlightenment*, New Jersey: Humanities Press

Kelchtermans, G. (1995) Teacher stress and burnout: reflections from a biographical perspective on teacher development, paper presented at Conference on Teacher Burnout, Marbach, November.

Kelchtermans, G. and Strittmatter, A. (1999) Beyond Individual Burnout: A Perspective for Improved Schools, Guidelines for the Prevention of Burnout, in Vandenberghe, R. and Huberman, A. M. *Understanding and Preventing Teacher Burnout*, Cambridge: Cambridge University Press.

Kemmis, S. (1988) Action research, in Keeves, J. P. (ed.) *Educational Research Methodology and Measurement: An International Handbook*, Oxford: Pergamon.

Kincheloe, J. L. (1991) *Teachers as Researchers: qualitative inquiry as a path to empowerment*, London: Falmer Press.

Kinder, K. and Harland, J. (1991) *The Impact of INSET: The Case of Primary Science*, Slough: NFER.

Konstlexicon A-L (The Encyclopaedia of Art A-L), Göteborg: AB Kulturhistoriska Förlagen.

Kuper, A. (1978/1987) *Anthropologists and Anthropology: The British School 1922-1972*, London: Routledge.

Kvale, S. (1996) *InterViews: An Introduction to Qualitative Research Interviewing*, London: Sage.

Lacey, C. (1970) *Hightown grammar*, Manchester: Manchester University Press.

Lacey, C. (1976) Problems of Sociological Fieldwork: a review of the methodology of 'Hightown Grammar, in Hammersley, M. and Woods, P. (eds) *The Process of Schooling*, London: Routledge and Kegan Paul.

Larsson, S. (1998) Om skolning av fältforskare, *Pedagogisk Forskning i Sverige*, 3(3):161-175.

Larsson, S. (2000) Skrivandets lust och olust, *Pedagogisk Forskning i Sverige*, 5(1): 30-42.

Lather, P. (1986) Research as praxis, *Harvard Educational Review*, 56(3): 257-77.

Lather, P. (1991) *Getting Smart: Feminist Research and Pedagogy with/in the Post-modern*, New York: Routledge.

Lather, P. (1997) Drawing the Line at Angels: working the ruins of feminist ethnography, *Qualitative Studies in Education*, 10(3): 285-304.

Lather, P. (2000) Ten years later, yet again: Critical pedagogy and its complicities, in Weiller, K and Stone, L. (eds) *Feminist Engagements: Revisioning Educational and Cultural Theory*, New York: Routledge.

Lather, P. and Smithies, C. (1997) *Troubling the Angels: women living with HIV/AIDS*, Boulder: Westview.

Lawn, M. (1988) Skill in schoolwork: work relations in the primary school, in: J. Ozga (ed.) *Schoolwork: approaches to the labour process of teaching* , Milton Keynes: Open University Press.

Lawn, M. and Grace. G. (eds) (1987) *Teachers: the Culture and politics of work*, Lewes: Falmer Press.

Lee, R. M. (1993) *Doing Research on Sensitive Topics*, London: Sage.

Liefooghe, A. (1999) Internet Mailbase Correspondence, July.

Mac an Ghaill, M. (1988) *Young, Gifted and Black: Student-teacher relations in the schooling of black youth*. Milton Keynes: Open University Press.

Mac an Ghaill, M. (1996a) Sociology of Education, State Schooling and Social Class: beyond critiques of the New Right hegemony, *British Journal of Sociology of Education*, 17(2): 163-176.

Mac an Ghaill, M. (1996b) Manufacturing Identities? Work, Self and the Primary School, paper presented at the *British Educational Research Association Conference*, University of Lancaster, September.

Maclure, M. (1993) Arguing for Your Self: identity as an organising principle in teachers' jobs and lives, *British Educational Research Journal*, 19(4): 311-322.

Marais-Steinman, S. (1999) Internet Mailbase Correspondence, July.

Marcus, G. (1998) *Ethnography through Thick and Thin: A New Research Imaginary for Athropology's Changing Professional Cultur*e, Princeton: Princeton University Press.

Marcus, G., and Fischer, M. J. (1986) *Anthropology as Cultural Critique*, Chicago: University of Chicago Press.

Marcuse, H. (1964) *One Dimensional Man*, London: Routledge and Kegan Paul.

Matza, D. and Sykes, G. M. (1957) Delinquency and subterranean values, *American Sociological Review*, 25(5): 712-719.

McCleod, D. and Meikle, J. (1994) Education reforms making heads quit, *The Guardian*, 1 September, p. 6.

Mead, G. H. (1934) *Mind, Self and Society*, Chicago: University of Chicago Press.

Measor, L. and Woods, P. (1991) Breakthroughs and Blockages in Ethnographic Research: Contrasting Experiences During the Changing Schools Project in Walford, G. (ed.) *Doing Educational Research*, London: Routledge.

Menter, I. and Pollard, A. (1989) The implications of the National Curriculum for reflective practice in initial teacher education, *Westminster Studies in Education*, 12: 31-42.

Menter, I., Muschamp, Y., Nicholls, P., Ozga, J. with Pollard, A. (1997) *Work and Identity in the Primary School*, Buckingham: Open University Press.

Mienczakowski, J. (1994) Reading and Writing Research, *NADIE Journal, (International Research Issue)*, 18: 45-54.

Mills, C. W. (1959)*The Sociological Imagination*, New York: Oxford University Press.

Moore, B. N., and Bruder, K. (1996) *Philosophy: The Power of Ideas*, Mountain View, California: Mayfield Press.

Mortimore, P., Mortimore, J., Thomas, H. (1994) *Managing Associate Staff in Primary and Secondary Schools*, London: Paul Chapman.

Mulkay, M. (1989) Textual fragments on science, social science and literature, in Mulkay, M. (1991) *Sociology of Science: A sociological pilgrimage*, Milton Keynes: Open University Press.

Nias, J. (1989) *Primary Teachers Talking: A study of teaching as work*, London: Routledge.

Nias, J. (1991b) Changing times, changing identities: Grieving for a lost self, in Burgess, R. G. (ed.) *Educational Research and Evaluation*, London: Falmer Press.

Nias, J., Southworth, G. and Campbell, P. (1992) *Whole School Curriculum Development in the Primary School*, London: Falmer Press.

Ofsted (1994) *Primary Matters: A discussion on teaching and learning in primary schools*, London: Ofsted.

Ofsted (1998) *Educational Research: A Critique*, London: Ofsted.

Osborn, M., Broadfoot, P., Pollard, A., Croll, P. and Abbott, D. (1994) Teachers' Professional Perspectives: Continuity and Change, paper presented as part of Symposium, Managing Change in the Primary School, *CEDAR International Conference*, University of Warwick, April.

Ozga, J. (1990) Policy Research and Policy Theory: a comment on Fitz and Halpin, *Journal of Education Policy*, 5(4): 359-362.

Paget, M. A. (1993) *A Complex Sorrow*, Philadelphia: Temple University Press.

Palmer, R. E. (1969) *Hermeneutics: Interpretation Theory in Schleiermacher, Dilthey, Heidegger and Gadamer*, Evanston: Northwestern University Press.

Parry, O. (1987) Uncovering the ethnographer, in McKeganey, N. P. and Cunningham-Burley, S. (eds) *Enter the Sociologist*, Aldershot: Avebury.

Pilhammar, E. (1991) *Det är vi som är dom: Sjuksköterskestuderandes föreställningar och perspektiv under utbildningstiden*. (Göteborg Studies in Educational Sciences 83), Göteborg: Acta Universitatis Gothoburgensis.

Pollard, A. (1982) Model of Coping Strategies, *British Journal of Sociology of Education*, 3(1): 19-37.

Pollard, A. (1984) Ethnography and Social Policy for Classroom Practice in Barton, L. and Walker, S. (eds), *Social Crisis and Educational Research*, Beckenham: Croom Helm.

Pollard, A. (1985) *The Social World of the Primary School*. London: Holt, Rinehart and Winston.

Pollard, A. (1990) Towards a sociology of learning in primary schools, *British Journal of Sociology of Education*, 11: 241-256.

Pollard, A. (1992) Teachers' Responses to the Reshaping of Primary Education, in Arnot, M. and Barton, L. (eds) *Voicing Concerns: sociological perspectives on contemporary education reforms*, Wallingford: Triangle Books.

Pollard, A., Broadfoot, P., Croll, P., Osborn, M. and Abbot, D. (1994) *Changing English Primary Schools: The Impact of the Education Reform Act at Key Stage One*, London: Cassell.

Pollard. A. and Tann. S. (1987) *Reflective Teaching in the Primary School: a handbook for the classroom*, London: Cassell.

Power, M. (1994) *The Audit Explosion*, London: Demos.

Power, S. (1996) *The Pastoral and the Academic: conflict and contradiction in the curriculum*, London: Cassell.

Rabinow, P. (1986) Representations are social facts: Modernity and post-modernity in anthropology, in Clifford, J and Marcus, G. (eds.) *Writing Culture: The Poetics and Politics of Ethnography*, Berkeley: University of California Press.

Reay, D. (1996) Micro-Politics in the 1990s: Staff Relationships in Secondary Schooling' paper presented at the *British Educational Research Association Conference*, University of Lancaster, September.

Reay, D. (1998) Setting the Agenda: the growing impact of market forces on pupil grouping in British Secondary Schooling, *Journal of Curriculum Studies*, 30(5): 545-558.

Reynolds, D. (1984) Relative autonomy reconstructed, in: Barton, L. and Walker, S. (eds) *Social Crisis and Educational Research*, London: Croom Helm.

Reynolds, D. (1998) Teacher Effectiveness: better teachers, better schools, *British Educational Research Association Newsletter*, October, No. 66(1): 26-29.

Richardson, L. (1990) *Writing Strategies: Reaching Diverse Audiences*, Newbury Park: Sage.

Richardson, L. (1992) The consequences of poetic representation: Writing the other, rewriting the self, in Ellis, C. and Flaherty, M. G. (eds) *Investigasting Subjectivity: Research on Lived Experience*, Newbury Park: Sage.

Richardson, L. (1994) Writing: A method of inquiry, in Denzin, N. and Lincoln, Y. (eds) *Handbook of Qualitative Research*, London and New York: Sage.

Rist, R. (1984) On the Application of Qualitative Research to the Policy Process: An Emergent Linkage, in Barton, L. and Walker, S. (eds) *Schools, Teachers and Teaching*, Lewes: Falmer Press.

Rist, R.C. (1980) Blitzkrieg ethnography: on the transformation of a method into a movement, *Educational Researcher*, 9(2): 8-10.

Roberts, H. (1981) *Doing Feminist Research*, London, Routledge Kegan Paul.

Rosenholtz, S. (1989) Workplace Conditions that Affect Quality and Commitment: Implications for Teacher Induction Programs, *The Elementary School Journal*, 89(4): 421-439.

Rudduck, J. and Nixon, J. (1992) School focussed research in case study mode, paper presented at *Symposium on Qualitative Data Analysis. British Educational Research Association Conference*, Stirling, September.

Säljö, R. (2000) *Lärande i praktiken: ett sociokulturellt perspektiv* (Learning in Practice: A Socio-Cultural Perspective), Stockholm: Prisma.

Sanjek, R. (1990) On ethnographic validity, in: Sanjek, R. (ed) *Fieldnotes—The Makings of Anthropology*, Ithaca and London: Cornell University Press.

Scheurich, J. J. (1997) *Research Method in the Postmodern*, London: Falmer Press.

Schwandt, (2000) Three epistemological stances for qualitative inquiry: Interpretivism, hermeneutics and social constructionism, in Denzin, N. K. and Lincoln, Y. S. (eds), *Handbook of Qualitative Research* (2nd Edition) London: Sage.

Seddon, T. (1998) Capacity building: A strategy for educating between state and market, paper presented at the Ethnography and Education Conference, University of Oxford.

Seremetakis, N. 1994. *The Senses Still: Perception and Memory as Material Culture of Modernity*, London: Westview Press.

Shaffir, W. B. and Stebbins, R, A. (eds) (1991) *Experiencing Fieldwork*, Newbury Park: Sage.

Shaffir, W. B., Stebbins, R. A., Turowetz, A. (eds) (1980) *Fieldwork Experience: qualitative approaches to social research*, New York: St Martin's.

Sharp, R. (1982) Self-contained ethnography or a science of phenomenal forms and inner relations, *Boston University Journal of Education*, 164(1): 48-63.

Siraj-Blatchford, J. and Siraj-Blatchford, I. (1995) *Educating The Whole Child: Cross Curricula Skills, Themes And Dimensions*, Buckingham: Open University Press.

Smith, D. (1987) *The Everyday World as Problematic: a feminist sociology*, Toronto: University of Toronto Press.

Snow, D. and Anderson L. (1987) Identity Work among the homeless: The Verbal Construction and Avowal of Personal Identities. *American Journal of Sociology* 92(6): 1336-1371.

Spivak, G. C. (1993) *Outside in the Teaching Machine*, London and New York: Routledge..

Sroufe, G. E. (1997) Improving the 'Awful Reputation' of Education Research, *Educational Researcher*, 26(7): 26-28.

Stanley, L. (ed.) (1990) *Feminist Praxis: research theory and epistemology in feminist sociology*, New York: Routledge Kegan Paul.

Stenhouse, L. (1975) *An Introduction to Curriculum Research and Development*, London: Heinemann.

Strauss, A. and Corbin, J. (1990) *Basics of qualitative research*, London: Sage.

Stronach, I. and Morris, B. (1994) Polemical notes on educational evaluation in the age of policy hysteria, *Evaluation and Research in Education*, 8(1 and 2): 5-19.

Stronach, I., Corbin, B., McNamara, O., Stark, S., and Warne, T. (2002) Towards an uncertain politics of professionalism: teacher and nurse identities in flux. *Journal of Education Policy*, 17(1): 109-138.

Taylor, V. (1998) Feminist Methodology, in *Social Movements Research, Qualitative Sociology*, 21(4): 357-380.

Tedlkock, B. (2000) Ethnography and Ethnographic representation, in Denzin, N. and Lincoln, Y. (eds), *Handbook of Qualitative Research* (2nd Edition), London: Sage.

The Guardian (1993) 4 November.

The Guardian (1994) No time for time out, 4 October.

Times Educational Supplement (1994) Head absent since angry meeting, 28 October.

Travers, C.J. and Cooper, C.L. (1996) *Teachers Under Pressure: Stress in the teaching profession*, London: Routledge.

Tritter, J. (1995) The Context of Educational Policy Research: changed constraints, new methodologies and ethical complexities, *British Journal of Sociology of Education*, 16(3): 419-430.

Troman, G. (1994) Headteachers, collaborative school cultures and school improvement: a changing relationship? paper prepared for the *British Educational Research Association Conference*, University of Oxford, September.

Troman, G. (1996) Models of the Good Teacher: defining and redefining teacher quality, in Woods, P. (ed.) *Contemporary Issues in Teaching and Learning*, Buckingham: Open University Press.

Troman, G. (1997) *The effects of restructuring on primary teachers' work: a sociological analysis*, PhD, Open University.

Troman, G. (2000) 'Teacher Stress in the Low-Trust Society', *British Journal of Sociology of Education*, (3): 331-353.

Troman, G., and Woods, P. (2001) *Primary teachers' stress*, London: Routledge Falmer.

Troyna, B. (1994) Blind Faith? Empowerment and Educational Research, paper presented at the *International Sociology of Education Conference*, University of Sheffield, January.

Troyna, B. (1994) The Everyday World of Teachers?: Deracialised discourses in the sociology of teachers and the teaching profession, *British Journal of Sociology of Education*, 15(3): 325-339.

Turner, V. (1982) From Ritual to Theatre, New York, *Performing Arts Journal Publications*.

Tyler, S. (1986) Post-modern ethnography: from document of the occult to occult document, in Clifford. J. and Marcus, G. (eds) *Writing, Culture*, Berkeley: University of California Press.

Tyler, S. A. (1987) *The Unspeakable: Discourse, Dialogue and Rhetoric in the post-Modern World*, Madison: University of Wisconsin Press.

Van Maanen, J. (1988) *Tales of the Field: On Writing Ethnography*, Chicago: University of Chicago Press.

Van Maanen, J. (1995) An end to innocence: The ethnography of ethnography, in Van Maanen, J. (ed.) *Representation in Ethnography*, London: Sage.

Vandenberghe, R. and Huberman, A. M. (1999) *Understanding and Preventing Teacher Burnout*, Cambridge: Cambridge University Press.

Viditch, A. J. and Lyman, S. M. (1994) Qualitative methods and their history in sociology and anthropology, in Denzin, N. and Lincoln, Y. (eds) *Handbook of Qualitative Research*, London and New York: Sage.

Walford, G. (ed.) (1991) *Doing Educational Research*, London: Routledge.

Walford, G. (ed.) (2002) Doing a doctorate in educational ethnograph,. *Studies in educational ethnography, Volume 7*, Oxford: Jai Press.

Walker, R. (1986) The conduct of educational case studies: ethics, theory and procedures, in Hammersley, H. (ed.) *Controversies in classroom research*, Milton Keynes: Open University Press.

Walker, R. and Adelman, C. (1972) *Towards a Sociography of Classrooms*, Final Report, SSRC Grants HR 1442/1, The Long-term Observation of Events Using Stop-Frame and Cinematography, Centre for Science Education, Chelsea College.

Watson, G. (1987) Make me reflexive-But not yet: Strategies for managing essential reflexivity in ethnographic discourse, *Anthropological Research*, 43(4): 162-178.

Webb, E. and Weick, K. E. (1983) Unobtrusive measures in organisation theory: a reminder, in Van Maanen, J. (ed.) *Qualitative Methodology*, Beverly Hills: Sage.

Webb, R. and Vulliamy, G. (1995) The changing role of the primary school curriculum co-ordinator, *The Curriculum Journal*, 6(1): 29-45, Spring.

Webb, R. and Vulliamy, G. (1996) *Roles and Responsibilities in the Primary School: changing demands, changing practices*, Buckingham: Open University Press.

Whitty, G. (1974) Sociology and the problem of radical educational change: towards a reconceptualization of the 'new' sociology of education, in Flude, M. and Ahier, J. (eds) *Educability Schools and Ideology*, London: Croom Helm.

Williams, R. (1976) Base and superstructure in Marxist cultural critique, in Dale, R. (ed.) *Schooling and Capitalism: A Sociological Reader*, London: Routledge and Kegan Paul.

Willis, P. (1977) *Learning to Labour: How Working Class Kids get Working Class Jobs*, Farnborough: Saxon House.

Willis, P. (1999) Labour power, culture and the cultural commodity, in Castells, M., Flecha, R., Freire, P., Giroux, H., Macedo, D. and Willis, P. (eds) *Critical Education in the New information Age*, Oxford: Rowman and Littlefield.

Wolcott, H.F. (1995) *The Art of Fieldwork*, London: Altamira.

Woods, P, (1986) *Inside Schools: Ethnography in Educational Research* London: Routledge.

Woods, P, and Jeffrey, B. (1998) Choosing Positions: Resolving the contradictions of Ofsted inspections, *British Journal of Sociology of Education* 19(4):547-570.

Woods, P. (1979) *The Divided School*, London, Routledge and Kegan Paul.

Woods, P. (1983) *Sociology and the School: An Interactionist Viewpoint*, London: Routledge and Kegan Paul

Woods, P. (1986) *Inside schools: Ethnography in educational research*, London: Routledge.

Woods, P. (1990) *Teacher skills and strategies*, London: Falmer.

Woods, P. (1993) *Critical events in teaching and learning*, London: Falmer Press.

Woods, P. (1995) *Creative teachers in primary schools*, Buckingham: Open University Press.

Woods, P. (1995) The Intensification of the Teacher's Self, presented at the Conference on *Teacher Burnout*, Marbach, November.

Woods, P. (1996) *Researching the art of teaching: ethnography for educational use*, London: Routledge.

Woods, P. (1996a) Research Proposal on Primary Teacher Stress and Burnout.

Woods, P. (1996b) *Researching the Art of Teaching: ethnography for educational use*, London: Routledge.

Woods, P. (1999a) Critical Moments in the Creative Teaching Research, in Walford, G. (ed.) *Doing Research About Education*, London: Falmer.

Woods, P. (1999b) Reconstructing Progressivism, Keynote Address to the *International Study Association on Teachers and Teaching*, 9th Biennial Conference, St. Patrick's College, Dublin, July.

Woods, P. (1999c) Personal Communication, August.

Woods, P. (2000) Isle of Wight School Journey: field notes. The Open University, Milton Keynes.

Woods, P. (forthcoming) Ethnographic Methods in the Creative Teaching Research in Gobbo, F. (ed.) *Etnografia dell'educazione in Europa*, Milan: Edizioni)

Woods, P. and Jeffrey, B. (1996) Teachable moments: the art of creative teaching in primary schools. Buckingham: Open University Press.

Woods, P. and Pollard, A. (eds) (1988) *Sociology and Teaching: a new challenge for the sociology of education*, Beckenham: Croom Helm.

Woods, P. and Wenham, P. (1995) Politics and Pedagogy: A Case Study in Appropriation, *Journal of Education Policy*, 10(2): 119-143.

Woods, P., Jeffrey, B., Troman, G., and Boyle, M. (1997) *Restructuring Schools, Reconstructing Teachers*, Buckingham: Open University Press.

Woods, P., Jeffrey, B., Troman, G. and Boyle, M. (1997) *Restructuring Schools, Reconstructing Teachers: Responding to Change in the Primary School*, Buckingham: Open University Press.

Woods. P. (1994a) Teachers under siege: resistance and appropriation in English primary schools, *Anthropology and Education Quarterly*, 25: 1-16.

Woods. P. (1994b) The dissemination of educational research through teachers, paper presented at St Hilda's at Warwick Conference, University of Warwick, September.

Woods. P. and Wenham, P. (1994) Teaching and researching the teaching of, a history topic: an experiment in collaboration, *The Curriculum Journal*, 5: 133-161.

Worsley, P. (ed.) (1970) *Introducing Sociology*, 2nd. edn., Harmondsworth:Penguin.

Wragg, E.C., Wragg, C.M., Haynes, G.S and Chamberlin, R.P. (1997) Teaching Competence Project, Occasional Paper 1, University of Exeter School of Education.

Printed in the United Kingdom
by Lightning Source UK Ltd.
111132UKS00002B/208-267